ELECTRICIAN SECOND YEAR MCQ

OBJECTIVE QUESTION ANSWERS

MANOJ DOLE

Digitization is the need of the time. In the future, training in industrial training institutes will need to be conducted using online internet to make training more convenient and easy. E-books containing a set of MCQ questions will be made available to the trainees as they need to be more accustomed to the multiple choice questions MCQ to prepare for the online exams taking place in their industrial training institutes.

With all these factors in mind, Mr. Manoj Madhukar Dole Instructor, Industrial Training Institute, Satara, has written books according to the new annual system and NSQF-5 syllabus. And they've created theoretical mobile apps and blogs to make training easier, and made all these educational materials available for download on the world famous websites Google Play Store, Amazon and Apple Book Store.

The books were published by Hon'ble Joint Director Shri Rajendra Ghume Saheb Regional Office of Vocational Education and Training, Pune on 9/1/2019, at this time Shri Prakash Saigavkar Saheb Principal Government Industrial Training Institute Aundh Pune, Shri Tukaram Misal Saheb Principal Govt. Q. Sanstha Satara, Shri Sachin Dhumal Saheb District Vocational Education and Training Officer Satara, Shri Yatin Pargaonkar Saheb Principal Govt. Q. Sanstha Kolhapur, Shri Vikas Teke Saheb Inspector Vocational Education and Training Regional Office Pune, Palekar Foods Products Pvt. Ltd. Entrepreneurial Chairman of Satara Mr. Nilkanthrao Palekar Saheb, Chairman of Hira Foods Mr. Ibrahim Baba Tamboli Saheb, Mrs. Shalmali Pawar Headmaster Government Technical School Center Satara and other dignitaries were present on the occasion.

Contents

Prologue

Electrician Second Year MCQ is a simple Book for ITI Engineering Course Electrician Second Year, NSQ F Syllabus in 2022, It contains objective questions with underlined & bold correct answers MCQ covering all topics including all about electrical rotating machines viz. DC machines, induction motors, alternators & MG sets and practice on them. The trainee will practice on determining characteristics, their performance analysis, starting, speed control and reversing direction of rotation of machines. He will practice on parallel operation & synchronization of alternators, winding practice and over hauling will be practiced for DC machine and induction motors. diodes for bridge rectifier, switching devices & amplifiers by electronic components, different wave shape generation and testing by CRO. Designing control cabinet, assembling control elements and their wiring are to be practiced. Speed control of AC/DC motors by electronic controller will be practiced. The trainee will practice on testing, analyzing and repairing of voltage stabilizer, emergency light, battery charger, UPS and inverter. He will gain knowledge of thermal, hydel, solar & wind energy systems. distribution system, domestic service line and accessories & their protection by practicing on relay and circuit breaker and lots more.

We add new question answers with each new version. Please email us in case of any errors/omissions. This is arguably the largest and best Book for All engineering multiple choice questions and answers.

As a student you can use it for your exam prep. This e-Book is also useful for professors to refresh material.

Foreword

Vocational education and training is imparted through the Department of Vocational Education and Training through the Department of Business Education and Business Practical to supply multi-skilled artisans in line with the rapidly growing demand in the industrial sector in the 21st century. All the occupations within the institutions are important, as the trainees from these occupations develop multi-skills as per the demands of the industry.

with the noble intention of making available MCQ e-books suitable for all businesses, considering that all the examinations in all the industries in the industrial sector are conducted online and include MCQ method questions. Mr. Manoj Madhukar Dole has written a very good e-book on MCQ method as per the new annual syllabus. This e-book will definitely be a guide for all the trainees, trainee candidates, training instructors and others concerned.

The author of the book is Mr. Manoj Madhukar Dole, Instructor Gov. ITI Satara has 17 years of training experience. Written as a new annual pattern, this e-book incorporates modern digital QR Code technology to understand the layout, simple language, and simple syntax, diagrams and videos for each subject. So I am sure that this e-book will definitely be useful for in-depth study and exam practice. The work they have done is certainly commendable.

Mr. Tukaram Misal
Principal Government Industrial Training Institute Satara

Preface

DGET New Delhi and CSTARI Kolkata have been implementing an annual pattern for all businesses in ITI since the August 2018 session. The examination system will also be changed and it will be online from this year and since all the questions are of Objective Type (MCQ), the trainees are in dire need of in-depth study. It is with this in mind that we are delighted to present the books based on the old NIMI pattern and a complete overview of the new annual pattern, and we hope that these books will be a guide for all business directors and trainees. Is.

For writing these books, Johar Awate Saheb, Principal of ITI Akluj. Former Principal of ITI Satara Saigavkar Saheb, Assistant Director Shri Chandrakant Dhekne Saheb Regional Office of Vocational Education and Training, Pune, District Vocational Education and Training Officer Sachin Dhumal Saheb and Headmaster Government Technical School Kendra Shalmali Pawar Madam and son Adhiraj Dole, mother Kusum Dole, I am very grateful to my father Madhukar Dole and wife Ashwini Dole for their special guidance and cooperation from time to time.

Also, in a very short period of time, the book was reviewed by Shri Rajendra Ghume Saheb, Joint Director, Vocational Education and Training Regional Office, Pune, for his invaluable time in publishing the book. I am sincerely grateful for their feedback.

I am grateful to the Instructor of ITI Satara for there continuous support from the very beginning of writing the book.

From this book, I consider myself blessed to have shared my thoughts on e-learning with you. I will not claim that this book is perfect, because considering the perfection, this book is an attempt and is in its infancy. They will be valuable for improvement if they are tested and suggested.

Manoj Dole
Dated 9/1/2019

Acknowledgements

The industrial training and theoretical examination system of our industrial training institutes and these changes have been accepted by the craft instructors and the trainees. Theoretical examinations conducted in your industrial training institutes are also conducted online. Since these examinations are of multiple choice MCQ method, the trainees will need to get more practice of such questions.

With all these considerations in mind, Mr. Manoj Madhukar, Director, Dole Crafts, Katari Industrial Training Institute, Satara, has done a thorough study and with his diligent work and added his keen intellect, according to the new annual system and NSQF-5 syllabus, e-book of Katari and other machine trades. -Book) and they have created mobile apps and blogs on theoretical topics to make training easier and have made all these educational materials available for download on the world famous websites Google Play Store, Amazon and Apple Book Store. Training has been made easier by creating a print version and using advanced techniques like QR Code.

All these educational materials will definitely be a guide for all the trainees for in-depth study and for the craft instructors and other concerned who are imparting vocational training.

CHAPTER ONE

Electrician Second Year QR Code Images for E-Learning

Download App
Online Test Exam
ITI Books
AutoCAD CAM
JOB & Apprentice
Online Theory
Computer Course
Trading Course
CNC Course
MSCIT Course
Shopping Business
Internet Business
Web Designing
Online Services
Top Sportsmans
Indian Army
Freedom Fighters
Top Scientists
Social Reformers
Motivational Speaker
Top Richest People
Join WhatsApp Group
Join Facebook Group
Like Facebook Page
PAN / Adhar / Licence Passport

14 ITi Book MCQ - Manoj Dole
www.itibook.com
battery
capacitor
cell
dynamometer
electromagnet
heater
inductance
magnet
www.itigov.blogspot.com www.jobapprentices.blogspot.com www.ititests.blogspot.com
www.itibook.com

15
ITI Book MCQ - Manoj Dole
www.itibook.com
megger
motor
multimeter
ohmmeter
resistores
star connected
alternator
voltmeter
ammeter
wattmeter
www.itigov.blogspot.com
www.jobapprentices.blogspot.com
www.ititests.blogspot.com
www.itibook.com

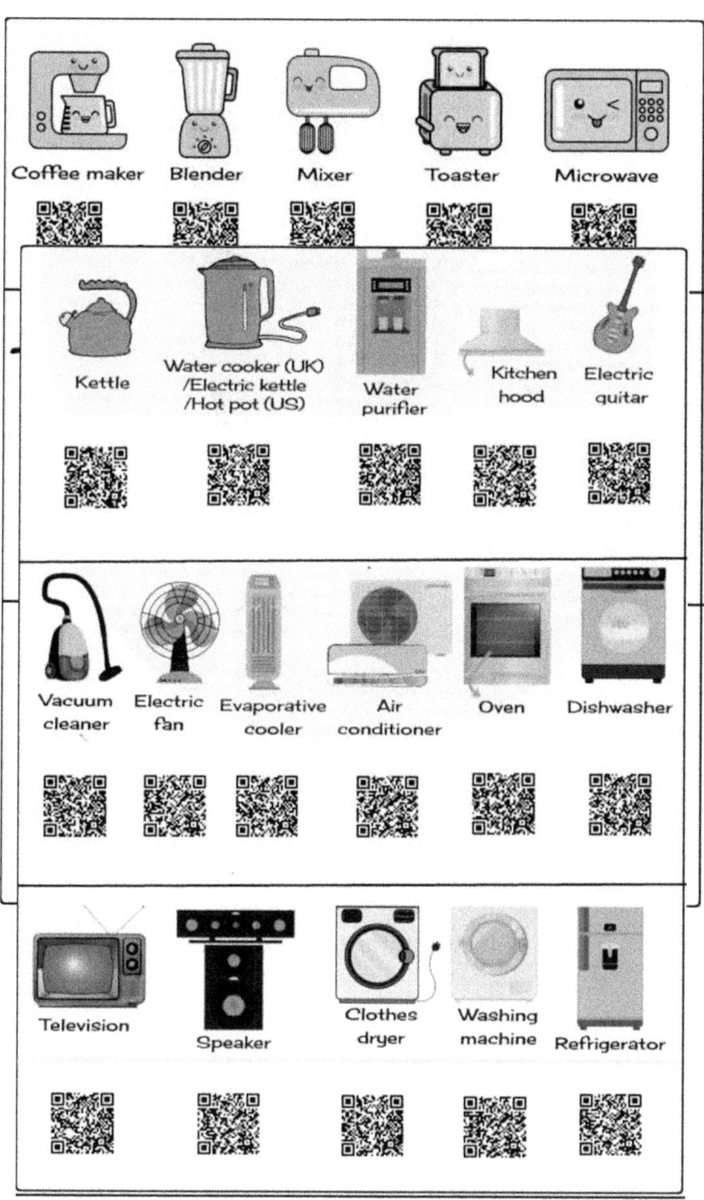
Coffee maker
Blender
Mixer
Toaster
Microwave
Kettle
Water cooker (UK)
/Electric kettle
/Hot pot (US)
Water
purifier
Kitchen
hood
Electric
guitar
Vacuum
cleaner
Electric
fan
Evaporative
cooler
Air
conditioner
Oven
Dishwasher
Television
Speaker
Clothes
dryer
Washing
machine
Refrigerator

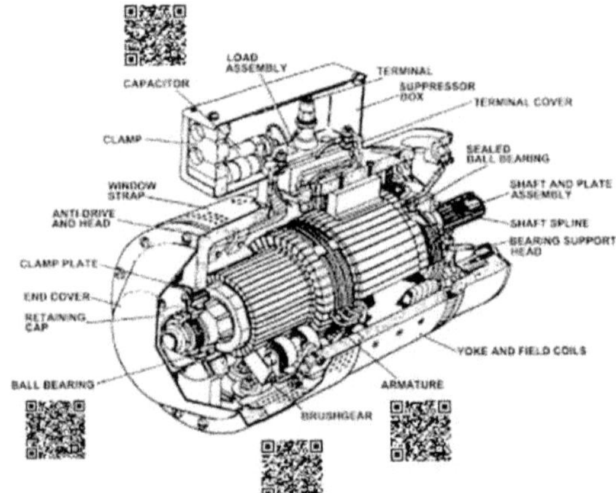

Electrical Generator

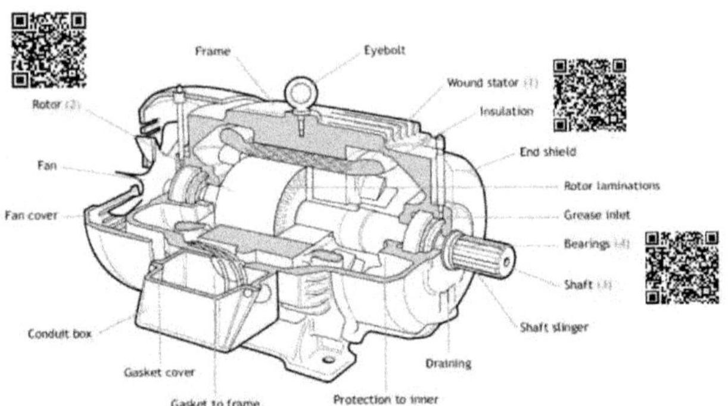

Electrical Induction Motor

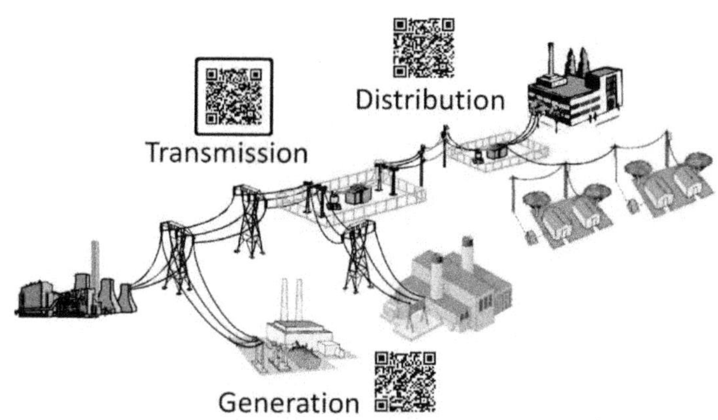

Electrical Power Distribution

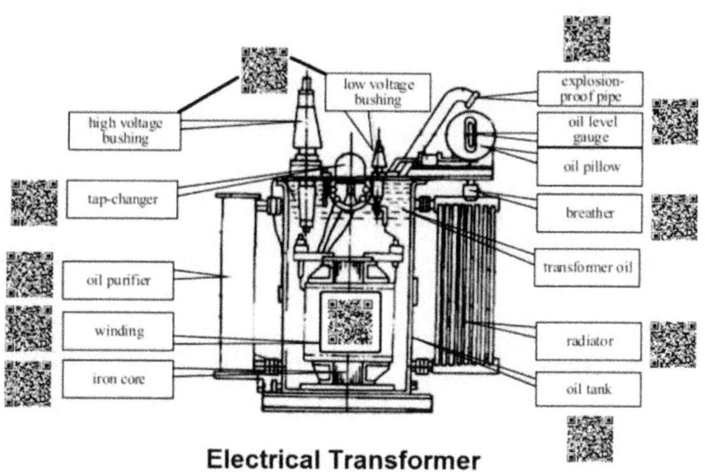

Electrical Transformer

CHAPTER TWO

Electrician Second Year MCQ

1. Laminations of core are generally made of

(a) case iron

(b) carbon

(c) silicon steel

(d) stainless steel

2. Which of the following could be lamina-proximately the thickness of laminations of a D.C. machine ?

(a) 0.005 mm

(b) 0.05 mm

(c) 0.5 m

(d) 5 m

3. The armature of D.C. generator is laminated to

(a) reduce the bulk

(b) provide the bulk

(c) insulate the core

(d) reduce eddy current loss

4. The resistance of armature winding depends on

(a) length of conductor

(b) cross-sectional area of the conductor

(c) number of conductors

(d) all of the above

5. The field coils of D.C. generator are usually made of

(a) mica

(b) copper

(c) cast iron

(d) carbon

6. The commutator segments are connected to the armature conductors by means of

(a) copper lugs
(b) resistance wires
(c) insulation pads
(d) brazing

7. In a commutator
(a) copper is harder than mica
(b) mica and copper are equally hard
(c) mica is harder than copper
(d) none of the above

8. In D.C. generators the pole shoes are fastened to the pole core by
(a) rivets
(b) counter sunk screws
(c) brazing
(d) welding

9. According to Fleming's right-hand rule for finding the direction of induced e.m.f., when middle finger points in the direction of induced e.m.f., forefinger will point in the direction of
(a) motion of conductor
(b) lines of force
(c) either of the above
(d) none of the above

10. Fleming's right-hand rule regarding direction of induced e.m.f., correlates
(a) magnetic flux, direction of current flow and resultant force
(b) magnetic flux, direction of motion and the direction of e.m.f. induced
(c) magnetic field strength, induced voltage and current
(d) magnetic flux, direction of force and direction of motion of conductor

11. While applying Fleming's right-hand rule to And the direction of induced e.m.f., the thumb points towards
(a) direction of induced e.m.f.
(b) direction of flux
(c) direction of motion of the conductor if forefinger points in the direction of generated e.m.f.
(d) direction of motion of conductor, if forefinger points along the lines of flux

12. The bearings used to support the rotor shafts are generally

(a) ball bearings
(b) bush bearings
(c) magnetic bearmgs
(d) needle bearings
13. In D.C. generators, the cause of rapid brush wear may be
(a) severe sparking
(b) rough commutator surface
(c) imperfect contact
(d) any of the above
14. In lap winding, the number of brushes is always
(a) double the number of poles
(b) same as the number of poles
(c) half the number of poles
(d) two
15. For a D.C. generator when the number of poles and the number of armature conductors is fixed, then which winding will give the higher e.m.f. ?
(a) Lap winding
(b) Wave winding
(c) Either of (a) and (b) above
(d) Depends on other features of design
16. In a four-pole D.C. machine
(a) all the four poles are north poles
(b) alternate poles are north and south
(c) all the four poles are south poles
(d) two north poles follow two south poles
17. Copper brushes in D.C. machine are used
(a) where low voltage and high currents are involved
(b) where high voltage and small cur-rents are involved
(c) in both of the above cases
(d) in none of the above cases
18. A separately excited generator as compared to a self-excited generator
(a) is amenable to better voltage control
(b) is more stable
(c) has exciting current independent of load current
(d) has all above features
19. In case of D.C. machines, mechanical losses are primary function of

(a) current
(b) voltage
(c) speed
(d) none of above
20. Iron losses in a D.C. machine are independent of variations in
(a) speed
(b) load
(c) voltage
(d) speed and voltage
21. In D.C. generators, current to the external circuit from armature is given through
(a) commutator
(b) solid connection
(c) slip rings
(d) none of above
23. Brushes of D.C. machines are made of
(a) carbon
(b) soft copper
(c) hard copper
(d) all of above
24. If B is the flux density, I the length of conductor and v the velocity of conductor, then induced e.m.f. is given by
(a)Blv
(b)Blv2
(c)Bl2v
(d)Bl2v2
25. In case of a 4-pole D.C. generator provided with a two layer lap winding with sixteen coils, the pole pitch will be
(a) 4
(b) 8
(c) 16
(d) 32
26. The material for commutator brushes is generally
(a) mica
(b) copper
(c) cast iron
(d) carbon

27. The insulating material used between the commutator segments is normally

(a) graphite

(b) paper

(c) mica

(d) insulating varnish

28. In D.C. generators, the brushes on commutator remain in contact with conductors which

(a) lie under south pole

(b) lie under north pole

(c) lie under interpolar region

(d) are farthest from the poles

29. If brushes of a D.C. generator are moved in order to bring these brushes in

magnetic neutral axis, there will be

(a) demagnetisation only

(b) cross magnetisation as well as mag¬netisation

(c) crossmagnetisation as well as demagnetising

(d) cross magnetisation only

30. Armature reaction of an unsaturated D.C. machine is

(a) crossmagnetising

(b) demagnetising

(c) magnetising

(d) none of above

31. D.C. generators are connected to the busbars or disconnected from them only under the floating condition

(a) to avoid sudden loading of the primemover

(b) to avoid mechanicaljerk to the shaft

(c) to avoid burning of switch contacts

(d) all above

32. Eddy currents are induced in the pole shoes of a D.C. machine due to

(a) oscillating magnetic field

(b) pulsating magnetic flux

(c) relative rotation between field and armature

(d) all above

34. Equilizer rings are required in case armature is

(a) wave wound

(b) lap wound

(c) delta wound
(d) duplex wound
35. Welding generator will have
(a) lap winding
(b) wave winding
(c) delta winding
(d) duplex wave winding
36. In case of D.C. machine winding, number of commutator segments is equal to
(a) number of armature coils
(b) number of armature coil sides
(c) number of armature conductors
(d) number of armature turns
37. For a D.C. machines laboratory following type of D.C. supply will be suitable
(a) rotary converter
(b) mercury are rectifier
(c) induction motor D.C. generator set
(d) synchronous motor D.C. generator set
38. The function of pole shoes in the case of D.C. machine is
(a) to reduce the reluctance of the mag¬netic path
(b) to spread out the flux to achieve uniform flux density
(c) to support the field coil
(d) to discharge all the above functions
Ans: d
39. In the case of lap winding resultant pitch is
(a) multiplication of front and back pitches
(b) division of front pitch by back pitch
(c) sum of front and back pitches
(d) difference of front and back pitches
40. A D.C. welding generator has
(a) lap winding
(b) wave moving
(c) duplex winding
(d) any of the above
41. Which of the following statement about D.C. generators is false ?
(a) Compensating winding in a D.C. machine helps in commutation

(b) In a D. C. generator interpoles winding is connected in series with the armature winding

(c) Back pitch and front pitch are both odd and approximately equal to the pole pitch

(d) Equilizing bus bars are used with parallel running of D.C. shunt generators

42. The demagnetising component of armature reaction in a D.C. generator

(a) reduces generator e.m.f.

(b) increases armature speed

(c) reduces interpoles flux density

(d) results in sparking trouble

43. Magnetic field in a D.C. generator is produced by

(a) electromagnets

(b) permanent magnets

(c) both (a) and (b)

(d) none of the above

44. The number of brushes in a commutator depends on

(a) speed of armature

(b) type of winding

(c) voltage

(d) amount of current to be collected

45. Compensating windings are used in D.C. generators

(a) mainly to reduce the eddy currents by providing local short-circuits

(b) to provide path for the circulation of cooling air

(c) to neutralise the cross-magnetising effect of the armature reaction

(d) none of the above

46. Which of the following components of a D.C, generator plays vital role for

providing direct current of a D.C. generator ?

(a) Dummy coils

(b) Commutator

(c) Eye bolt

(d) Equilizer rings

47. In a D.C. generator the ripples in the direct e.m.f. generated are reduced by

(a) using conductor of annealed copper

(b) using commutator with large number of segments

(c) using carbon brushes of superior quality
(d) using equiliser rings

48. In D.C. generators, lap winding is used for
(a) high voltage, high current
(b) low voltage, high current
(c) high voltage, low current
(d) low voltage, low current

49. Two generators A and B have 6-poles each. Generator A has wave wound armature while generator B has lap wound armature. The ratio of the induced e.m.f. is generator A and B will be
(a) 2 : 3
(b) 3 : 1
(c) 3 : 2
(d) 1 : 3

50. The voltage drop for which of the following types of brush can be expected to be least ?
(a) Graphite brushes
(b) Carbon brushes
(c) Metal graphite brushes
(d) None of the above

51. The e.m.f. generated by a shunt wound D.C. generator isE. Now while pole flux remains constant, if the speed of the generator is doubled, the e.m.f. generated will be
(a) E/2
(b) 2E
(c) slightly less than E
(d) E

53. The armature core of a D.C. generator is usually made of
(a) silicon steel
(b) copper
(c) non-ferrous material
(d) cast-iron

54. Satisfactory commutation of D.C. machines requires
(a) brushes should be of proper grade and size
(b) brushes should smoothly run in the holders
(c) smooth, concentric commutator properly undercut
(d) all of the above

54a. Open circuited armature coil of a D.C. machine is

(a) identified by the scarring of the commutator segment to which open circuited coil is connected

(b) indicated by a spark completely around the commutator

(c) both (a) and (b)

(d) none of the above

56. For the parallel operation of two or more D.C. compound generators, we

should ensure that

(a) voltage of the incoming generator should be same as that of bus bar

(b) polarity of incoming generator should be same as that of bus bar

(c) all the series fields should be run in parallel by means of equilizer connection

(d) series fields of all generators should be either on positive side or negative side of the armature

57. D.C. series generator is used

(a) to supply traction load

(b) to supply industrial load at constant voltage

(c) voltage at the toad end of the feeder

(d) for none of the above purpose

58. Following D.C. generator will be in a position to build up without any residual magnetism in the poles

(a) series generator

(b) shunt generator

(c) compound generator

(d) self-excited generator

59. Interpole flux should be sufficient to

(a) neutralise the commutating self induced e.m.f.

(b) neutralise the armature reaction flux

(c) neutralise both the armature reaction flux as well as commutating e.m.f. induced in the coil

(d) perform none of the above functions

60. D.C. generator generally preferred for charging automobile batteries is

(a) series generator

(b) shunt generator

(c) long shunt compound generator

(d) any of'the above

61. In a D.C. generator the number of mechanical degrees and electrical degrees will be the same when

(a) r.p.m. is more than 300

(b) r.p.m. is less than 300

(c) number of poles is 4

(d) number of poles is 2

62. Permeance is the reciprocal of

(a) flux density

(b) reluctance

(c) ampere-turns

(d) resistance

63. In D.C. generators the polarity of the interpoles

(a) is the same as that of the main pole ahead

(b) is the same as that of the immediately preceding pole

(c) is opposite to that of the main pole ahead

(d) is neutral as these poles do not play part in generating e.m.f.

64. The e.m.f. generated in a D.C. generator is directly proportional to

(a) flux/pole

(b) speed of armature

(c) number of poles

(d) all of the above

65. In a D.C. generator the magnetic neutral axis coincides with the geometrical neutral axis, when

(a) there is no load on the generator

(b) the generator runs on full load

(c) the generator runs on overload

(d) the generator runs on designed speed

66. In a D.C. generator in order to reduce sparking at brushes, the self-induced e.m.f. in the coil is neutralised by all of the following except

(a) interpoles

(b) dummy coils

(c) compensating winding

(d) shifting of axis of brushes

67. In D.C. generators on no-load, the air gap flux distribution in space is

(a) sinusoidal

(b) triangular

(c) pulsating

(d) flat topped

68. A shunt generator running at 1000 r.p.m. has generated e.m.f. as 200 V. If the speed increases to 1200 r.p.m., the generated e.m.f. will be nearly

(a) 150 V

(b) 175 V

(c) 240 V

(d) 290 V

69. The purpose of providing dummy coils in a generator is

(a) to reduce eddy current losses

(b) to enhance flux density

(c) to amplify voltage

(d) to provide mechanical balance for the rotor

1. No-load speed of which of the following motor will be highest ?

(a) Shunt motor

(b) Series motor

(c) Cumulative compound motor

(d) Differentiate compound motor

2. The direction of rotation of a D.C. series motor can be changed by

(a) interchanging supply terminals

(b) interchanging field terminals

(c) either of (a) and (b) above

(d) None of the above

3. Which of the following application requires high starting torque ?

(a) Lathe machine

(b) Centrifugal pump

(c) Locomotive

(d) Air blower

4. If a D.C. motor is to be selected for conveyors, which rriotor would be preferred ?

(a) Series motor

(b) Shunt motor

(c) Differentially compound motor

(d) Cumulative compound motor

5. Which D.C. motor will be preferred for machine tools ?

(a) Series motor

(b) Shunt motor

(c) Cumulative compound motor

(d) Differential compound motor

6. Differentially compound D.C. motors can find applications requiring

(a) high starting torque
(b) low starting torque
(c) variable speed
(d) frequent on-off cycles
7. Which D.C. motor is preferred for elevators ?
(a) Shunt motor
(b) Series motor
(c) Differential compound motor
(d) Cumulative compound motor
8. According to Fleming's left-hand rule, when the forefinger points in the direction of the field or flux, the middle finger will point in the direction of
(a) current in the conductor aovtaat of conductor
(c) resultant force on conductor
(d) none of the above
9. If the field of a D.C. shunt motor gets opened while motor is running
(a) the speed of motor will be reduced %
(b) the armature current will reduce
(c) the motor will attain dangerously high speed 1
(d) the motor will continue to nuvat constant speed
10. Starters are used with D.C. motors because
(a) these motors have high starting torque
(b) these motors are not self-starting
(c) back e.m.f. of these motors is zero initially
(d) to restrict armature current as there is no back e.m.f. while starting
11. In D.C. shunt motors as load is reduced
(a) the speed will increase abruptly
(b) the speed will increase in proportion to reduction in load
(c) the speed will remain almost/constant
(d) the speed will reduce
12. A D.C. series motor is that which
(a) has its field winding consisting of thick wire and less turns
(b) has a poor torque
(c) can be started easily without load
(d) has almost constant speed
13. For starting a D.C. motor a starter is required because
(a) it limits the speed of the motor
(b) it limits the starting current to a safe value

(c) it starts the motor

(d) none of the above

14. The type of D.C. motor used for shears and punches is

(a) shunt motor

(b) series motor

(c) differential compoutid D.C. motor

(d) cumulative compound D.C. motor

15. If a D.C. motor is connected across the A.C. supply it will

(a) run at normal speed

(b) not run

(c) run at lower speed

(d) burn due to heat produced in the field winding by .eddy currents

16. To get the speed of D.C, motor below the normal without wastage of electrical energy is used.

(a) Ward Leonard control

(b) rheostatic control

(c) any of the above method

(d) none of the above method

17. When two D.C. series motors are connected in parallel, the resultant speed is

(a) more than the normal speed

(b) loss than the normal speed

(c) normal speed

(d) zero

18. The speed of a D.C. shunt motor more than its full-load speed can be obtained by

(a) decreasing the field current

(b) increasing the field current

(c) decreasing the armature current

(d) increasing the armature current

19. In a D.C. shunt motor, speed is

(a) independent of armature current

(b) directly proportional to the armature current

(c) proportional to the square of the current

(d) inversely proportional to the armature current

20. A direct on line starter is used: for starting motors

(a) up to 5 H.P.

(b) up to 10 H.P.

(c) up to 15 H.P.

(d) up to 20 H.P.

21. What will happen if the back e.m.f. of a D.C. motor vanishes suddenly?

(a) The motor will stop

(b) The motor will continue to run

(c) The armature may burn

(d) The motor will run noisy

22. In case of D.C. shunt motors the speed is dependent on back e.m.f. only because

(a) back e.m.f. is equal to armature drop

(b) armature drop is negligible

(c) flux is proportional to armature current

(d) flux is practically constant in D:C. shunt motors

23. In a D.C. shunt motor, under the conditions of maximum power, the current in the armature will be

(a) almost negligible

(b) rated full-load current

(c) less than full-load current

(d) more than full-load current

24. These days D.C. motors are widely used in

(a) pumping sets

(b) air compressors

(c) electric traction

(d) machine shops

25. By looking at which part of the motor, it can be easily confirmed that a particular motor is D.C. motor?

(a) Frame

(b) Shaft

(c) Commutator

(d) Stator

26. In which of the following applications D.C. series motor is invariably tried?

(a) Starter for a car

(b) Drive for a water pump

(c) Fan motor

(d) Motor operation in A.C. or D.C.

27. In D.C. machines fractional pitch winding is used

(a) to improve cooling
(b) to reduce copper losses
(c) to increase the generated e.m.f.
(d) to reduce the sparking

28. A three point starter is considered suitable for
(a) shunt motors
(b) shunt as well as compound motors
(c) shunt, compound and series motors
(d) all D.C. motors

29. In case-the conditions for maximum power for a D.C. motor are established, the efficiency of the motor will be
(a) 100%
(b) around 90%
(c) anywhere between 75% and 90%
(d) less than 50%

30. The ratio of starting torque to full-load torque is least in case of
(a) series motors
(b) shunt motors
(c) compound motors
(d) none of the above

31. In D.C. motor which of the following can sustain the maximum temperature rise?
(a) Slip rings
(b) Commutator
(c) Field winding
(d) Armature winding

33. Which of the following law/rule can he used to determine the direction of rotation of D.C. motor ?
(a) Lenz's law
(b) Faraday's law
(c) Coloumb's law
(d) Fleming's left-hand rule

34. Which of the following load normally needs starting torque more than the rated torque?
(a) Blowers
(b) Conveyors
(c) Air compressors
(d) Centrifugal pumps

35. The starting resistance of a D.C. motor is generally

(a) low

(b) around 500 Q

(c) 1000 Q

(d) infinitely large

36. The speed of a D.C. series motor is

(a) proportional to the armature current

(b) proportional to the square of the armature current

(c) proportional to field current

(d) inversely proportional to the armature current

37. In a D.C. series motor, if the armature current is reduced by 50%, the torque of the motor will be equal to

(a) 100% of the previous value

(b) 50% of the previous value

(c) 25% of the previous value

(d) 10% of the previous value

38. The current drawn by the armature of D.C. motor is directly proportional to

(a) the torque required

(b) the speed of the motor

(c) the voltage across the terminals

(d) none of the above

39. The power mentioned on the name plate of an electric motor indicates

(a) the power drawn in kW

(b) the power drawn in kVA

(c) the gross power

(d) the output power available at the shaft

40. Which D.C. motor has got maximum self loading property?

(a) Series motor

(b) Shunt motor

(c) Cumulatively compounded ‘motor

(d) Differentially compounded motor

41. Which D.C. motor will be suitable along with flywheel for intermittent light and heavy loads?

(a) Series motor

(b) Shunt motor

(c) Cumulatively compounded motor

(d) Differentially compounded motor

42. If a D.C. shunt motor is working at no load and if shunt field circuit suddenly opens

(a) nothing will happen to the motor

(b) this will make armature to take heavy current, possibly burning it

(c) this will result in excessive speed, possibly destroying armature due to excessive centrifugal stresses

(d) motor will run at very slow speed

43. D.C. series motors are used

(a) where load is constant

(b) where load changes frequently

(c) where constant operating speed is needed

(d) in none of the above situations.

44. For the same H.P. rating and full load speed, following motor has poor starting torque

(a) shunt

(b) series

(c) differentially compounded

(d) cumulativelyc'ompounded

45. In case of conductively compensated D.C. series motors, the compensating winding is provided

(a) as separately wound unit

(6) in parallel with armature winding

(c) in series with armature winding

(d) in parallel with field winding

46. Sparking at the commutator of a D.C. motor may result in

(a) damage to commutator segments

(b) damage to commutator insulation

(c) increased power consumption

(d) all of the above

47. Which of the following motor is preferred for operation in highly explosive atmosphere ?

(a) Series motor

(b) Shunt motor

(c) Air motor

(d) Battery operated motor

48. If the supply voltage for a D.C. motor is increased, which of the following will decrease ?

(a) Starting torque
(b) Operating speed
(c) Full-load current
(d) All of the above

49. Which one of the following is not the function of pole shoes in a D.C. machine ?

(a) To reduce eddy current loss
(b) To support the field coils
(c) To spread out flux for better uniformity
(d) To reduce the reluctance of the magnetic path

50. The mechanical power developed by a shunt motor will be maximum when the ratio of back e.m.f. to applied voltage is

(a) 4.0
(b) 2.0
(c) 1.0
(d) 0.5

51. The condition for maximum power in case of D.C. motor is

(a) back e.m.f. = 2 x supply voltage
(b) back e.m.f. = | x supply voltage
(c) supply voltage = | x back e.m.f.
(d) supply voltage = back e.m.f.

52. For which of the following applications a D.C. motor is preferred over an A.C. motor ?

(a) Low speed operation
(b) High speed operation
(c) Variable speed operation
(d) Fixed speed operation

53. In D.C. machines the residual magnetism is of the order of

(a) 2 to 3 per cent
(6) 10 to 15 per cent
(c) 20 to 25 per cent
(d) 50 to 75 per cent

54. Which D.C. motor is generally preferred for cranes and hoists ?

(a) Series motor
(b) Shunt motor
(c) Cumulatively compounded motor
(d) Differentially compounded motor

55. Three point starter can be used for

(a) series motor only

(b) shunt motor only

(c) compound motor only

(d) both shunt and compound motor

56. Sparking, is discouraged in a D.C. motor because

(a) it increases the input power con-sumption

(b) commutator gets damaged

(c) both (a) and (b)

(d) none of the above

57. Speed control by Ward Leonard method gives uniform speed variation

(a) in one direction

(b) in both directions

(c) below normal speed only

(d) above normal speed only.

58. Flywheel is used with D.C. compound motor to reduce the peak demand by the motor, compound motor will have to be

(a) level compounded

(b) under compounded

(c) cumulatively compounded

(d) differentially compounded

59. Following motor is used where high starting torque and wide speed range control is required.

(a) Single phase capacitor start

(b) Induction motor

(c) Synchronous motor

(d) D.C. motor

60. In a differentially compounded D.C. motor, if shunt field suddenly opens

(a) the motor will first stop and then run in opposite direction as series motor

(b) the motor will work as series motor and run at slow speed in the same direction

(c) the motor will work as series motor and run at high speed in the same direction

(d) the motor will not work and come to stop

61. Which of the following motor has the poorest speed regulation ?

(a) Shunt motor

(b) Series motor

(c) Differential compound motor

(d) Cumulative compound motor

62. Buses, trains, trolleys, hoists, cranes require high starting torque and therefore make use of

(a) D.C. series motor

(b) D.C. shunt motor

(c) induction motor

(d) all of above motors

63. As -the load is increased the speed of D.C. shunt motor will

(a) reduce slightly

(b) increase slightly

(c) increase proportionately

(d) remains unchanged

64. The armature torque of the D.C. shunt motor is proportional to

(a) field flux only

(b) armature current only

(c) both (a) and (b)

(d) none of the above

65. Which of the following method of speed control of D.C. machine will offer minimum efficiency ?

(a) Voltage control method

(b) Field control method

(c) Armature control method

(d) All above methods

1. Which of the following component is usually fabricated out of silicon steel ?

(a) Bearings

(b) Shaft

(c) Statorcore

(d) None of the above

2. The frame of an induction motor is usually made of

(a) silicon steel

(b) cast iron

(c) aluminium

(d) bronze

3. The shaft of an induction motor is made of

(a) stiff

(b) flexible

(c) hollow

(d) any of the above

4. The shaft of an induction motor is made of

(a) high speed steel

(b) stainless steel

(c) carbon steel

(d) cast iron

5. In an induction motor, no-load the slip is generally

(a) less than 1%

(b) 1.5%

(c) 2%

(d) 4%

6. In medium sized induction motors, the slip is generally around

(a) 0.04%

(b) 0.4%

(c) 4%

(d) 14%

7. In squirrel cage induction motors, the rotor slots are usually given slight skew

in order to

(a) reduce windage losses

(b) reduce eddy currents

(c) reduce accumulation of dirt and dust

(d) reduce magnetic hum

8. In case the air gap in an induction motor is increased

(a) the magnetising current of the rotor will decrease

(b) the power factor will decrease

(c) speed of motor will increase

(d) the windage losses will increase

9. Slip rings are usually made of

(a) copper

(b) carbon

(c) phospor bronze

(d) aluminium

10. A 3-phase 440 V, 50 Hz induction motor has 4% slip. The frequency of rotor

e.m.f. will be

(a) 200 Hz
(b) 50 Hz
(c) 2 Hz
(d) 0.2 Hz

11. In Ns is the synchronous speed and s the slip, then actual running speed of an
induction motor will be
(a) Ns
(b) s.N,
(c) (l-s)Ns
(d) (Ns-l)s

The efficiency of an induction motor can be expected to be nearly
(a) 60 to 90%
(b) 80 to 90%
(c) 95 to 98%
(d) 99%

13. The number of slip rings on a squirrel cage induction motor is usually
(a) two
(b) three
(c) four
(d) none

14. The starting torque of a squirrel-cage induction motor is
(a) low
(b) negligible
(c) same as full-load torque
(d) slightly more than full-load torque

15. A double squirrel-cage induction motor has
(a) two rotors moving in oppsite direction
(b) two parallel windings in stator
(c) two parallel windings in rotor
(d) two series windings in stator

16. Star-delta starting of motors is not possible in case of
(a) single phase motors
(b) variable speed motors
(c) low horse power motors
(d) high speed motors

17. The term 'cogging' is associated with
(a) three phase transformers

(b) compound generators
(c) D.C. series motors
(d) induction motors
18. In case of the induction motors the torque is
(a) inversely proportional to (Vslip)
(b) directly proportional to (slip)2
(c) inversely proportional to slip
(d) directly proportional to slip
19. An induction motor with 1000 r.p.m. speed will have
(a) 8 poles
(b) 6 poles
(c) 4 poles
(d) 2 poles
20. The good power factor of an induction motor can be achieved if the average
flux density in the air gap is
(a) absent
(b) small
(c) large
(d) infinity
21. An induction motor is identical to
(a) D.C. compound motor
(b) D.C. series motor
(c) synchronous motor
(d) asynchronous motor
22. The injected e.m.f. in the rotor of induction motor must have
(a) zero frequency
(b) the same frequency as the slip frequency
(c) the same phase as the rotor e.m.f.
(d) high value for the satisfactory speed control
23. Which of the following methods is easily applicable to control the speed of the
squirrel-cage induction motor ?
(a) By changing the number of stator poles
(b) Rotor rheostat control
(c) By operating two motors in cascade
(d) By injecting e.m.f. in the rotor circuit
24. The crawling in the induction motor is caused by

(a) low voltage supply
(b) high loads
(c) harmonics develped in the motor
(d) improper design of the machine
(e) none of the above

25. The auto-starters (using three auto transformers) can be used to start cage
induction motor of the following type
(a) star connected only
(b) delta connected only
(c) (a) and (b) both
(d) none of the above

26. The torque developed in the cage induction motor with autostarter is
(a) k/torque with direct switching
(6) K x torque with direct switching
(c) K2 x torque with direct switching
(d) k2/torque with direct switching

27. When the equivalent circuit diagram of doouble squirrel-cage induction motor
is constructed the two cages can be
considered
(a) in series
(b) in parallel
(c) in series-parallel
(d) in parallel with stator

28. It is advisable to avoid line-starting of induction motor and use starter
because
(a) motor takes five to seven times its full load current
(b) it will pick-up very high speed and may go out of step
(c) it will run in reverse direction
(d) starting torque is very high

29. Stepless speed control of induction motor is possible by which of the following methods ?
(a) e.m.f. injection in rotor eueuit
(b) Changing the number of poles
(c) Cascade operation
(d) None of the above

30. Rotor rheostat control method of speed control is used for
(a) squirrel-cage induction motors only
(b) slip ring induction motors only
(c) both (a) and (b)
(d) none of the above

31. In the circle diagram for induction motor, the diameter of the circle represents
(a) slip
(b) rotor current
(c) running torque
(d) line voltage

32. For which motor the speed can be controlled from rotor side ?
(a) Squirrel-cage induction motor
(b) Slip-ring induction motor
(c) Both (a) and (b)
(d) None of the above

33. If any two phases for an induction motor are interchanged
(a) the motor will run in reverse direction
(b) the motor will run at reduced speed
(c) the motor will not run
(d) the motor will burn

34. An induction motor is
(a) self-starting with zero torque
(b) self-starting with high torque
(c) self-starting with low torque
(d) non-self starting

35. The maximum torque in an induction motor depends on
(a) frequency
(b) rotor inductive reactance
(c) square of supply voltage
(d) all of the above

36. In three-phase squirrel-cage induction motors
(a) rotor conductor ends are short-circuited through slip rings
(b) rotor conductors are short-circuited through end rings
(c) rotor conductors are kept open
(d) rotor conductors are connected to insulation

37. In a three-phase induction motor, the number of poles in the rotor winding is always

(a) zero
(b) more than the number of poles in stator
(c) less than number of poles in stator
(d) equal to number of poles in stator

38. DOL starting of induction motors is usually restricted to
(a) low horsepower motors
(b) variable speed motors
(c) high horsepower motors
(d) high speed motors

39. The speed of a squirrel-cage induction motor can be controlled by all of the
following except
(a) changing supply frequency
(b) changing number of poles
(c) changing winding resistance
(d) reducing supply voltage

40. The 'crawling" in an induction motor is caused by
(a) high loads
(6) low voltage supply
(c) improper design of machine
(d) harmonics developed in the motor

41. The power factor of an induction motor under no-load conditions will be
closer to
(a) 0.2 lagging
(b) 0.2 leading
(c) 0.5 leading
(d) unity

42. The 'cogging' of an induction motor can be avoided by
(a) proper ventilation
(b) using DOL starter
(c) auto-transformer starter
(d) having number of rotor slots more or less than the number of stator slots (not equal)

43. If an induction motor with certain ratio of rotor to stator slots, runs at 1/7 of the normal speed, the phenomenon will be termed as
(a) humming
(b) hunting

(c) crawling

(d) cogging

44. Slip of an induction motor is negative when

(a) magnetic field and rotor rotate in opposite direction

(b) rotor speed is less than the synchronous speed of the field and are in the same direction

(c) rotor speed is more than the synchronous speed of the field and are in the same direction

(d) none of the above

45. Size of a high speed motor as compared to low speed motor for the same H.P. will be

(a) bigger

(b) smaller

(c) same

(d) any of the above

46. A 3-phase induction motor stator delta connected, is carrying full load and one of its fuses blows out. Then the motor

(a) will continue running burning its one phase

(b) will continue running burning its two phases

(c) will stop and carry heavy current causing permanent damage to its winding

(d) will continue running without any harm to the winding

47. A 3-phase induction motor delta connected is carrying too heavy load and oneof its fuses blows out. Then the motor

(a) will continue running burning its one phase

(b) will continue running burning its two phase

(c) will stop and carry heavy current causing permanent damage to its winding

(d) will continue running without any harm to the winding

48. Low voltage at motor terminals is due to

(a) inadequate motor wiring

(b) poorely regulated power supply

(c) any one of the above

(d) none of the above

49. In an induction motor the relationship between stator slots and rotor slots is that

(a) stator slots are equal to rotor slots

(b) stator slots are exact multiple of rotor slots

(c) stator slots are not exact multiple of rotor slots

(d) none of the above

50. Slip ring motor is recommended where

(a) speed control is required

(6) frequent starting, stopping and reversing is required

(c) high starting torque is needed

(d) all above features are required

51. As load on an induction motor goes on increasing

(a) its power factor goes on decreasing

(b) its power factor remains constant

(c) its power factor goes on increasing even after full load

(d) its power factor goes on increasing up to full load and then it falls again

52. If a 3-phase supply is given to the stator and rotor is short circuited rotor will move

(a) in the opposite direction as the direction of the rotating field

(b) in the same direction as the direction of the field

(c) in any direction depending upon phase squence of supply

53. It is advisable to avoid line starting of induction motor and use starter because

(a) it will run in reverse direction

(b) it will pick up very high speed and may go out of step

(c) motor takes five to seven times its full load current

(d) starting torque is very high

54. The speed characteristics of an induction motor closely resemble the speedload characteristics of which of the following machines

(a) D.C. series motor

(b) D.C. shunt motor

(c) universal motor

(d) none of the above

55. Which type of bearing is provided in small induction motors to support the rotor shaft ?

(a) Ball bearings

(b) Cast iron bearings

(c) Bush bearings

(d) None of the above

56. A pump induction motor is switched on to a supply 30% lower than its rated voltage. The pump runs. What will eventually happen ? It will

(a) stall after sometime
(b) stall immediately
(c) continue to run at lower speed without damage
(d) get heated and subsequently get damaged

57. 5 H.P., 50-Hz, 3-phase, 440 V, induction motors are available for the following r.p.m. Which motor will be the costliest ?
(a) 730 r.p.m.
(b) 960 r.p.m.
(c) 1440 r.p.m.
(d) 2880 r.p.m.

58. A 3-phase slip ring motor has
(a) double cage rotor
(b) wound rotor
(c) short-circuited rotor
(d) any of the above

59. The starting torque of a 3-phase squirrel cage induction motor is
(a) twice the full load torque
(b) 1.5 times the full load torque
(c) equal to full load torque

60. Short-circuit test on an induction motor cannot be used to determine
(a) windage losses
(b) copper losses
(c) transformation ratio
(d) power scale of circle diagram

61. In a three-phase induction motor
(a) iron losses in stator will be negligible as compared to that in rotor
(6) iron losses in motor will be neg¬ligible as compared to that in rotor
(c) iron losses in stator will be less than that in rotor
(d) iron losses in stator will be more than that in rotor

62. In case of 3-phase induction motors, plugging means
(a) pulling the motor directly on line without a starter
(b) locking of rotor due to harmonics
(c) starting the motor on load which is more than the rated load
(d) interchanging two supply phases for quick stopping

63. Which is of the following data is required to draw the circle diagram for an induction motor ?
(a) Block rotor test only
(b) No load test only

(c) Block rotor test and no-load test

(d) Block rotor test, no-load test and stator resistance test

64. In three-phase induction motors sometimes copper bars are placed deep in the rotor to

(a) improve starting torque

(b) reduce copper losses

(c) improve efficiency

(d) improve power factor

65. In a three-phase induction motor

(a) power factor at starting is high as compared to that while running

(b) power factor at starting is low as compared to that while running

(c) power factor at starting in the same as that while running

66. The vafcie of transformation ratio of an induction motor can be found by

(a) open-circuit test only

(b) short-circuit test only

(c) stator resistance test

(d) none of the above

67. The power scale of circle diagram of an induction motor can be found from

(a) stator resistance test

(b) no-load test only

(c) short-circuit test only

(d) noue of the above

68. The shape of the torque/slip curve of induction motor is

(a) parabola

(b) hyperbola

(c) rectangular parabola

(d) straigth line

69. A change of 4% of supply voltage to an induction motor will produce a change of appromimately

(a) 4% in the rotor torque

(b) 8% in the rotor torque

(c) 12% in the rotor torque

(d) 16% in the rotor torque

70. The stating torque of the slip ring induction motor can be increased by adding

(a) external inductance to the rotor

(b) external resistance to the rotor

(c) external capacitance to the rotor

(d) both resistance and inductance to rotor

71. A 500 kW, 3-phase, 440 volts, 50 Hz, A.C. induction motor has a speed of 960 r.p.m. on full load. The machine has 6 poles. The slip of the machine will be

(a) 0.01

(b) 0.02

(c) 0.03

(d) 0.04

72. The complete circle diagram of induetion motor can be drawn with the help of

data found from

(a) noload test

(6) blocked rotor test

(c) stator resistance test

(d) all of the above

73. In the squirrel-cage induction motor the rotor slots are usually given slight skew

(a) to reduce the magnetic hum and locking tendency of the rotor

(b) to increase the tensile strength of the rotor bars

(c) to ensure easy fabrication

(d) none of the above

74. The torque of a rotor in an induction motor under running condition is maximum

(a) at the unit value of slip

(b) at the zero value of slip

(c) at the value of the slip which makes rotor reactance per phase equal to the resistance per phase

(d) at the value of the slip which makes the rotor reactance half of the rotor

75. What will happen if the relative speed between the rotating flux of stator and rotor of the induction motor is zero ?

(a) The slip of the motor will be 5%

(b) The rotor will not run

(c) The rotor will run at very high speed

(d) The torque produced will be very large

76. The circle diagram for an induction motor cannot be used to determine

(a) efficiency

(b) power factor

(c) frequency

(d) output

77. Blocked rotor test on induction motors is used to find out

(a) leakage reactance

(b) power factor on short circuit

(c) short-circuit current under rated voltage

(d) all of the above

78. Lubricant used for ball bearing is usually

(a) graphite

(b) grease

(c) mineral oil

(d) molasses

79. An induction motor can run at synchronous speed when

(a) it is run on load

(b) it is run in reverse direction

(c) it is run on voltage higher than the rated voltage

(d) e.m.f. is injected in the rotor circuit

80. Which motor is preferred for use in mines where explosive gases exist ?

(a) Air motor

(b) Induction motor

(c) D.C. shunt motor

(d) Synchronous motor

81. The torque developed by a 3-phase induction motor least depends on

(a) rotor current

(b) rotor power factor

(c) rotor e.m.f.

(d) shaft diameter

82. In an induction motor if air-gap is increased

(a) the power factor will be low

(b) windage losses will be more

(c) bearing friction will reduce

(d) copper loss will reduce In an induction motor

83. In induction motor, percentage slip depends on

(a) supply frequency
(b) supply voltage
(c) copper losses in motor
(d) none of the above

85. In case of a double cage induction motor, the inner cage has
(a) high inductance arid low resistance
(b) low inductance and high resistance
(c) low inductance and low resistance
(d) high inductance and high resistance

86. The low power factor of induction motor is due to
(a) rotor leakage reactance
(b) stator reactance
(c) the reactive lagging magnetizing current necessary to generate the magnetic flux
(d) all of the above

87. Insertion of reactance in the rotor circuit
(a) reduces starting torque as well as maximum torque
(b) increases starting torque as well as maximum torque
(c) increases starting torque but maxi-mum torque remains unchanged
(d) increases starting torque but maxi-mum torque decreases

88. Insertion of resistance in the rotcir of an induction motor to develop a given torque
(a) decreases the rotor current
(b) increases the rotor current
(c) rotor current becomes zero
(d) rotor current rernains same

89. For driving high inertia loods best type of induction motor suggested is
(a) slip ring type
(b) squirrel cage type
(c) any of the above
(d) none of the above

90. Temperature of the stator winding of a three phase induction motor is

obtained by
(a) resistance rise method
(b) thermometer method
(c) embedded temperature method

(d) all above methods

91. The purpose of using short-circuit gear is

(a) to short circuit the rotor at slip rings

(b) to short circuit the starting resistances in the starter

(c) to short circuit the stator phase of motor to form star

(d) none of the above

92. In a squirrel cage motor the induced e.m.f. is

(a) dependent on the shaft loading

(b) dependent on the number of slots

(c) slip times the stand still e.m.f. induced in the rotor

(d) none of the above

93. Less maintenance troubles are experienced in case of

(a) slip ring induction motor

(b) squirrel cage induction motor

(c) both (a) and (b)

(d) none of the above

94. A squirrel cage induction motor is not selected when

(a) initial cost is the main consideration

(b) maintenance cost is to be kept low

(c) higher starting torque is the main consideration

(d) all above considerations are involved

95. Reduced voltage starter can be used with

(a) slip ring motor only but not with squirrel cage induction motor

(b) squirrel cage induction motor only but not with slip ring motor

(c) squirrel cage as well as slip ring induction motor

(d) none of the above

96. Slip ring motor is preferred over squirrel cage induction motor where

(a) high starting torque is required

(b) load torque is heavy

(c) heavy pull out torque is required

(d) all of the above

97. In a star-delta starter of an induction motor

(a) resistance is inserted in the stator

(b) reduced voltage is applied to the stator

(c) resistance is inserted in the rotor

(d) applied voltage perl stator phase is 57.7% of the line voltage

98. The torque of an induction motor is

(a) directly proportional to slip

(b) inversely proportional to slip
(c) proportional to the square of the slip
(d) none of the above

99. The rotor of an induction motor runs at
(a) synchronous speed
(b) below synchronous speed
(c) above synchronous speed
(d) any of the above

100. The starting torque of a three phase induction motor can be increased by
(a) increasing slip
(b) increasing current
(c) both (a) and (b)
(d) none of the above

1. Synchronous motors are generally not self-starting because
(a) the direction of rotation is not fixed
(b) the direction of instantaneous torque reverses after half cycle
(c) startes cannot be used on these machines
(d) starting winding is not provided on the machines

2. In case one phase of a three-phase synchronous motor is short-circuited the motor will
(a) not start
(b) run at 2/3 of synchronous speed
(c) run with excessive vibrations
(d) take less than the rated load

3. A pony motor is basically a
(a) small induction motor
(b) D.C. series motor
(c) D.C. shunt motor
(d) double winding A.C./D.C. motor

4. A synchronous motor can develop synchronous torque
(a) when under loaded
(b) while over-excited
(c) only at synchronous speed
(d) below or above synchronous speed

5. A synchronous motor can be started by
(a) pony motor
(b) D.C. compound motor

(c) providing damper winding

(d) any of the above

6. A three-phase synchronous motor will have

(a) no slip-rings

(b) one slip-ring

(c) two slip-rings

(d) three slip-rings

7. Under which of the following conditions hunting of synchronous motor is likely to occur ?

(a) Periodic variation of load

(b) Over-excitation

(c) Over-loading for long periods

(d) Small and constant load

8. When the excitation of an unloaded salient pole synchronous motor suddenly gets disconnected

(a) the motor stops

(b) it runs as a reluctance motor at the same speed

(c) it runs as a reluctance motor at a lower speed

(d) none of the above

9. When V is the applied voltage, then the breakdown torque of a synchronous motor varies as

(a) V

(b) V312

(c) V2

(d) 1/V

10. The power developed by a synchronous motor will be maximum when the load angle is

(a) zero

(b) 45°

(c) 90°

(d) 120°

11. A synchronous motor can be used as a synchronous capacitor when it is

(a) under-loaded

(b) over-loaded

(c) under-excited

(d) over-excited

12. A synchronous motor is running on a load with normal excitation. Now if the load on the motor is increased

(a) power factor as well as armature current will decrease

(b) power factor as well as armature current will increase

(c) power factor will increase but armature current will decrease

(d) power factor will decrease and armature current will increase

13. Mostly, synchronous motors are of

(a) alternator type machines

(6) induction type machines

(c) salient pole type machines

(d) smooth cylindrical type machines

14. The synchronous motor is not inherently self-starting because

(a) the force required to accelerate the rotor to the synchronous speed in an instant is absent

(b) the starting device to accelerate the rotor to near synchronous speed is absent

(c) a rotating magnetic field does not have enough poles

(d) the rotating magnetic field is produced by only 50 Hz frequency currents

15. As the load is applied to a synchronous motor, the motor takes more armature current because

(a) the increased load has to take more current

(b) the rotor by shifting its phase backward causes motor to take more current

(c) the back e.m.f. decreases causing an increase in motor current

(d) the rotor strengthens the rotating field casuing more motor current

16. Synchronous motor always runs at

(a) the synchronous speed

(b) less than synchronous speed

(c) more than synchronous speed

(d) none of the above

17. An over-excited synchronous motor takes

(a) leading current

(b) lagging current

(c) both (a) and (b)

(d) none of the above

18. The working of a synchronous motor is similar to

(a) gear train arrangement

(b) transmission of mechancial power by shaft
(c) distribution transformer
(d) turbine
(e) none of the above

19. The minimum armature current of the synchronous motor corresponds to operation at
(a) zero power factor leading
(b) unity power factor
(c) 0.707 power factor lagging
(d) 0.707 power factor leading

20. In a synchronous motor, the magnitude of stator back e.m.f. £& depends on
(a) d.c. excitation only
(b) speed of the motor
(c) load on the motor
(d) both the speed and rotor flux

21. If load (or torque) angle of a 4-pole synchronous motor is 6° electrical, its
value in mechanical degrees is
(a) 2
(b) 3
(c) 4
(d) 6

22. For V-curves for a synchronous motor the graph is drawn between
(a) field current and armature current
(b) terminal voltage and load factor
(c) power factor and field current
(d) armature current and power factor

23. The back e.m.f. of a synchronous motor depends on
(a) speed
(b) load
(c) load angle
(d) all of the above

24. A synchronous motor can operate at
(a) lagging power factor only
(6) leading power factor only
(c) unity power factor only
(d) lagging, leading and unity power factors

25. In a synchronous motor which loss varies with load ?
(a) Windage loss
(b) Bearing friction loss
(c) Copper loss
(d) Core loss

26. A synchronous motor can be made self starting by providing
(a) damper winding on rotor poles
(b) damper winding on stator
(c) damper winding on stator as well as rotor poles
(d) none of the above

27. The oscillations in a synchronous motor can be damped out by
(a) maintaining constant excitation
(b) running the motor on leading power factors
(c) providing damper bars in the rotor pole faces
(d) oscillations cannot be damped

28. The shaft of synchronous motor is made of
(a) mild steel
(b) chrome steel
(c) alnico
(d) stainless steel

29. When the field of a synchronous motor is under-excited, the power factor will be
(a) leading
(b) lagging
(c) unity
(d) zero

30. The speed regulation of a synchronous motor is always
(a) 1%
(b) 0.5%
(c) positive
(d) zero

31. The percentage slip in case of a synchronous motor is
(a) 1%
(b) 100%
(c) 0.5%
(d) zero

32. The operating speed of a synchronous motor can be changed to new fixed value by

(a) changing the load
(b) changing the supply voltage
(c) changing frequency
(d) using brakes

33. A synchronous motor will always stop when
(a) supply voltage fluctuates
(b) load in motor varies
(c) excitation winding gets disconnected
(d) supply voltage frequency changes9885859805

34. riunting in a synchronous motor takes place
(a) when supply voltage fluctuates
(b) when load varies
(c) when power factor is unity
(d) motor is under loaded

35. When load on an over-excited or under excited synchronous*motor is increased, rate of change of its armature current as compared with that of power factor is
(a) more
(b) less
(c) equal
(d) twice

36. The rotor copper losses, in a synchronous motor, are met by
(a) d.c. source
(b) armature input
(c) motor input
(d) supply lines

37. The maximum power developed in a synchronous motor occurs at a coupling angle of
(a) 30°
(b) 60°
(c) 90°
(d) 180°

38. When the stator windings are connected in such a fashion that the number of poles are made half, the speed of the rotor of a synchronous motor
(a) remains same as the original value
(b) decreases to half the original value
(c) tends to becomes zero

(d) increases to two times the original value

39. In which of the following motors the stator and rotor magnetic field rotate at

the same speed ?

(a) Universal motor

(b) Synchronous motor

(c) Induction motor

(d) Reluctance motor

40. Synchronsizingpower of a synchronous machine is

(a) direcly proportional to the synchronous reactance

(b) inversely proportional to the synchronous reactance

(a) equal to the synchronous reactance

(d) none of the above

41. Synchronous motors are

(a) not-self starting

(b) self-starting

(c) essentially self-starting

(d) none of the above

42. The standard full-load power factor ratings for synchronous motors are

(a) zero or 0.8 leading

(b) unity or 0.8 lagging

(c) unity or 0.8 leading

(d) unity or zero

43. A synchronous motor running with normal excitation adjusts to load increases essentially by increase in

(a) back e.m.f.

(b) armature current

(c) power factor

(d) torque angle

44. A synchronous motor has better power factor as compared to that of an equivalent induction motor. This is mainly because

(a) synchronous motor has no slip

(b) stator supply is not required to produce magnetic field

(c) mechanical load on the rotor remains constant

(d) synchronous motor has large airgap

45. A synchronous motor working at leading power factor can be used as

(a) voltage booster

(b) phase advancer

(c) noise generator

(d) mechanical synchronizer

46. Slip rings are usually made of

(a) carbon or graphite

(b) brass or steel

(c) silver or gold

(d) copper or aluminium

47. An over excited synchronous motor is used for

(a) fluctuating loads

(b) variable speed loads

(c) low torque loads

(d) power factor corrections

48. When the voltage applied to a synchronous motor is increased, which of the following will reduce ?

(a) Stator flux

(b) Pull in torque

(c) Both (a) and (b)

(d) None of the above

51. The efficiency of a properly designed synchronous motor will usually fall in range

(a) 60 to 70%

(b) 75 to 80%

(c) 85 to 95%

(d) 99 to 99.5%

52. To limit the operating temperature an electrical machine should have proper

(a) voltage rating

(b) current rating

(c) power factor

(d) speed

53. Slip-rings in a synchronous motor carry

(a) direct current

(b) alternating current

(c) no current

(d) all of the above

54. A synchronous machine with large air gap has

(a) a higher value of stability limit

(6) a small value of inherent regulation

(c) a higher synchronizing power which makes the machine less sensitive to load variations

(d) all of the above

55. The armature current of the synchronous motor has higher values for

(a) high excitation only

(b) low excitation only

(c) both (a) and (b)

(d) none of the above

56. In a synchronous motor running with fixed excitation, when the load is increased three times, its torque angle becomes approximately

(a) one-third

(b) twice

(c) thrice

(d) six times

57. The angle between the rotating stator flux and rotor poles is called ______ angle.

(a) torque

(b) obtuse

(c) synchronizing

(d) power factor

58. Which of the following methods is used to start a synchronous motor ?

(a) Damper winding

(b) Star-delta starter

(c) Damper winding in conjunction with star-delta starter

(d) Resistance starter in the armature circuit

59. When the rotor speed, in a synchronous machine, becomes more than the synchronous speed during hunting, the damper bars develop

(a) inductor motor torque

(b) induction generator torque

(c) synchronous motor torque

(d) d.c. motor toque

60. An important advantage of a synchronous motor over wound round induction motor is that

(a) its power factor may be varied at will

(b) its speed is independent of supply frequency

(c) its speed may be controlled more easily

(d) none of the above

61. The mechanical displacement of the rotor with respect to the stator, in polyphase multipolar synchronous motors running at full load, is of the order of

(a) zero degree

(b) two degrees

(c) five degrees

(d) ten degrees

62. Power factor of a synchronous motor is unity when

(a) the armature current is maximum

(b) the armature current is minimum

(c) the armature current is zero

(d) none of the above

63. Change of D.C. excitation of a synchronous motor changes

(a) applied voltage of the motor

(b) motor speed

(c) power factor of power drawn by the motor

(d) any of the above

(e) all of the above

64. While starting a synchronous motor by induction motor action, field winding is usually

(a) connected to D.C. supply

(b) short-circuited by low resistance

(c) kept open-circuited

(d) none of the above

1. The property of coil by which a counter e.m.f. is induced in it when the current

through the coil changes is known as

(a) self-inductance

(b) mutual inductance

(c) series aiding inductance

(d) capacitance

2. As per Faraday's laws of electromagnetic induction, an e.m.f. is induced in a

conductor whenever it

(a) lies perpendicular to the magnetic flux

(b) lies in a magnetic field

(c) cuts magnetic flux

(d) moves parallel to the direction of the magnetic field

3. Which of the following circuit element stores energy in the electromagnetic
field ?

(a) Inductance

(b) Condenser

(c) Variable resistor

(d) Resistance

4. The inductance of a coil will increase under all the following conditions except

(a) when more length for the same number of turns is provided

(6) when the number of turns of the coil increase

(c) when more area for each turn is provided

(d) when permeability of the core increases

5. Higher the self-inductance of a coil,

(a) lesser its weber-turns

(b) lower the e.m.f. induced

(c) greater the flux produced by it

(d) longer the delay in establishing steady current through it

6. In an iron cored coil the iron core is removed so that the coil becomes an air cored coil. The inductance of the coil will

(a) increase

(b) decrease

(c) remain the same

(d) initially increase and then decrease

7. An open coil has

(a) zero resistance and inductance

(b) infinite resistance and zero inductance

(c) infinite resistance and normal inductance

(d) zero resistance and high inductance

8. Both the number of turns and the core length of an inductive coil are doubled.

Its self-inductance will be

(a) unaffected

(b) doubled

(c) halved

(d) quadrupled

9. If current in a conductor increases then according to Lenz's law self-induced

voltage will

(a) aid the increasing current

(b) tend to decrease the amount of cur-rent

(c) produce current opposite to the in-creasing current

(d) aid the applied voltage

10. The direction of induced e.m.f. can be found by

(a) Laplace's law

(b) Lenz's law

(c) Fleming's right hand rule

(d) Kirchhoff s voltage law

11. Air-core coils are practically free from

(a) hysteresis losses

(b) eddy current losses

(c) both (a) and (b)

(d) none of the above

12. The magnitude of the induced e.m.f. in a conductor depends on the

(a) flux density of the magnetic field

(b) amount of flux cut

(c) amount of flux linkages

(d) rate of change of flux-linkages

13. Mutually inductance between two magnetically-coupled coils depends on

(a) permeability of the core

(b) the number of their turns

(c) cross-sectional area of their common core

(d) all of the above

14. A laminated iron core has reduced eddy-current losses because

(a) more wire can be used with less D.C. resistance in coil

(b) the laminations are insulated from each other

(c) the magnetic flux is concentrated in the air gap of the core

(d) the laminations are stacked vertfcally

15. The law that the induced e.m.f. and current always oppose the cause producing them is due to

(a) Faraday

(b) Lenz

(c) Newton

16. Which of the following is not a unit of inductance ?
(a) Henry
(b) Coulomb/volt ampere
(c) Volt second per ampere
(d) All of the above
17. In case of an inductance, current is proportional to
(a) voltage across the inductance
(b) magnetic field
(c) both (a) and (b)
(d) neither (a) nor (b)
18. Which of the following circuit elements will oppose the change in circuit
current ?
(a) Capacitance
(b) Inductance
(c) Resistance
(d) All of the above
19. For a purely inductive circuit which of the following is true ?
(a) Apparent power is zero
(b) Relative power is.zero
(c) Actual power of the circuit is zero
(d) Any capacitance even if present in the circuit will not be charged
20. Which of the following is unit of inductance ?
(a) Ohm
(b) Henry
(c) Ampere turns
(d) Webers/metre
21. An e.m.f. of 16 volts is induced in a coil of inductance 4H. The rate of change
of current must be
(a) 64 A/s
(b) 32 A/s
(c) 16 A/s
(d) 4 A/s
22. The core of a coil has a length of 200 mm. The inductance of coil is 6 mH. If
the core length is doubled, all other quantities, remaining the same, the inductance will be

(a) 3 mH
(b) 12 mH
(c) 24mH
(d)48mH

23. The self inductances of two coils are 8 mH and 18 mH. If the co-efficients of
coupling is 0.5, the mutual inductance of the coils is
(a) 4 mH
(b) 5 mH
(c) 6 mH
(d) 12 mH

24. Two coils have inductances of 8 mH and 18 mH and a co-efficient of coupling
of 0.5. If the two coils are connected in series aiding, the total inductance will be
(a) 32 mH
(b) 38 mH
(c) 40 mH
(d) 48 mH

25. A 200 turn coil has an inductance of 12 mH. If the number of turns is
increased to 400 turns, all other quantities (area, length etc.) remaining the same,
the inductance will be
(a) 6 mH
(b) 14 mH
(c) 24 mH
(d) 48 mH

26. Two coils have self-inductances of 10 H and 2 H, the mutual inductance being
zero. If the two coils are connected in series, the total inductance will be
(a) 6 H
(b) 8 H
(c) 12 H
(d) 24 H

27. In case all the flux from the current in coil 1 links with coil 2, the co-efficient
of coupling will be

(a) 2.0
(b) 1.0
(c) 0.5
(d) zero

28. A coil with negligible resistance has 50V across it with 10 mA. The inductive reactance is
(a) 50 ohms
(b) 500 ohms
(c) 1000 ohms
(d) 5000 ohms

29. A conductor 2 meters long moves at right angles to a magnetic field of flux density 1 tesla with a velocity of 12.5 m/s. The induced e.m.f. in the conductor will be
(a) 10 V
(6) 15 V
(c) 25V
(d) 50V

30. Lenz's law is a consequence of the law of conservation of
(a) induced current
(b) charge
(c) energy
(d) induced e.m.f.

31. A conductor carries 125 amperes of current under 60° to a magnetic field of 1.1 tesla. The force on the conductor will be nearly
(a) 50 N
(b) 120 N
(c) 240 N
(d) 480 N

32. Find the force acting on a conductor 3m long carrying a current of 50 amperes at right angles to a magnetic field having a flux density of 0.67 tesla.
(a) 100 N
(b) 400 N

(c) 600 N

(d) 1000 N

33. The co-efficient of coupling between two air core coils depends on

(a) self-inductance of two coils only

(b) mutual inductance between two coils only

(c) <u>mutual inductance and self inductance of two coils</u>

(d) none of the above

34. An average voltage of 10 V is induced in a 250 turns solenoid as a result of a

change in flux which occurs in 0.5 second. The total flux change is

(a) 20 Wb

(b) 2 Wb

(c) 0.2 Wb

(d) <u>0.02 Wb</u>

35. A 500 turns solenoid develops an average induced voltage of 60 V. Over what

time interval must a flux change of 0.06 Wb occur to produce such a voltage ?

(a) 0.01 s

(b) 0.1 s

(c) <u>0.5 s</u>

(d) 5 s

36. Which of the fpllowing inductor will have the least eddy current losses ?

(a) <u>Air core</u>

(b) Laminated iron core

(c) Iron core

(d) Powdered iron core

37. A coil induces 350 mV when the current changes at the rate of 1 A/s. The

value of inductance is

(a) 3500 mH

(b) <u>350 mH</u>

(c) 250 mH

(d) 150 mH

38. Two 300 uH coils in series without mutual coupling have a total inductance of

(a) 300 uH

(b) 600 uH

(c) 150 uH

(d) 75 uH

39. Current changing from 8 A to 12 A in one second induced 20 volts in a coil.

The value of inductance is

(a) 5 mH

(b) 10 mH

(c) 5 H

(d) 10 H

40. Which circuit element(s) will oppose the change in circuit current ?

(a) Resistance only

(b) Inductance only

(c) Capacitance only

(d) Inductance and capacitance

41. A crack in the magnetic path of an inductor will result in

(a) unchanged inductance

(b) increased inductance

(c) zero inductance

(d) reduced inductance

42. A coil is wound on iron core which carries current I. The self-induced voltage

in the coil is not affected by

(a) variation in coil current

(b) variation in voltage to the coil

(c) change of number of turns of coil

(d) the resistance of magnetic path

1. An air gap is usually inserted in magnetic circuits to

(a) increase m.m.f.

(b) increase the flux

(c) prevent saturation

(d) none of the above

2. The relative permeability of a ferromagnetic material is

(a) less than one

(b) more than one

(c) more than 10

(d) more than 100 or 1000

3. The unit of magnetic flux is

(a) henry
(b) weber
(c) ampereturn/weber
(d) ampere/metre

4. Permeability in a magnetic circuit corresponds to______ in an electric circuit.

(a) resistance
(b) resistivity
(c) conductivity
(d) conductance

5. Point out the wrong statement.

Magnetic leakage is undesirable in electric machines because it

(a) lowers their power efficiency
(b) increases their cost of manufacture
(c) leads to their increased weight
(d) produces fringing

6. Relative permeability of vacuum is

(a) 1
(b) 1 H/m
(c) 1/4JI
(d) 4n x 10-‘ H/m

7. Permanent magnets are normally made of

(a) alnico alloys
(b) aluminium
(c) cast iron
(d) wrought iron

8. Energy stored by a coil is doubled when its current is increased by percent.

(a) 25
(b) 50
(c)41.4
(d) 100

9. Those magnetic materials are best suited for making armature and transformer

cores which have____permeability and________hystersis loss.

(a) high, high
(b) low, high
(c) high, low

(d) low, low

10. The rate of rise of current through an inductive coil is maximum

(a) at 63.2% of its maximum steady value

(b) at the start of the current flow

(c) after one time constant

(d) near the final maximum value of current

11. When both the inductance and resistance of a coil are doubled the value of

(a) time constant remains unchanged

(b) initial rate of rise of current is doubled

(c) final steady current is doubled

(d) time constant is halved

12. The initial rate of rise of current through a coil of inductance 10 H when

suddenly connected to a D.C. supply of 200 V is________Vs

(a) 50

(b) 20

(c) 0.05

(d) 500

13. A material for good magnetic memory should have

(a) low hysteresis loss

(b) high permeability

(c) low retentivity

(d) high retentivity

14. Conductivity is analogous to

(a) retentivity

(b) resistivity

(c) permeability

(d) inductance

15. In a magnetic material hysteresis loss takes place primarily due to

(a) rapid reversals of its magnetisation

(b) flux density lagging behind magnetising force

(c) molecular friction

(d) it high retentivity

16. Those materials are well suited for making permanent magnets which have

______ retentivity and ________ coercivity.

(a) low, high

(b) high, high
(c) high, low
(d) low, low
17. If the area of hysteresis loop of a material is large, the hysteresis loss in this
material will be
(a) zero
(b) small
(c) large
(d) none of the above
18. Hard steel is suitable for making permanent magnets because
(a) it has good residual magnetism
(b) its hysteresis loop has large area
(c) its mechanical strength is high
(d) its mechanical strength is low
19. Silicon steel is used in electrical machines because it has
(a) low coercivity
(b) low retentivity
(c) low hysteresis loss
(d) high coercivity
20. Conductance is analogous to
(a) permeance
(b) reluctance
(c) flux
(d) inductance
21. The property of a material which opposes the creation of magnetic flux in it is
known as
(a) reluctivity
(b) magnetomotive force
(c) permeance
(d) reluctance
22. The unit of retentivity is
(a) weber
(b) weber/sq. m
(c) ampere turn/meter
(d) ampere turn
23. Reciprocal of reluctance is

(a) reluctivity
(b) permeance
(c) permeability
(d) susceptibility
24. While comparing magnetic and electric circuits, the flux of magnetic circuit is
compared with which parameter of electrical circuit ?
(a) E.m.f.
(b) Current
(c) Current density
(d) Conductivity
25. The unit of reluctance is
(a) metre/henry
(b) henry/metre
(c) henry
(d) 1/henry
26. A ferrite core has less eddy current loss than an iron core because
(a) ferrites have high resistance
(b) ferrites are magnetic
(c) ferrites have low permeability
(d) ferrites have high hysteresis
27. Hysteresis loss least depends on
(a) volume of material
(b) frequency
(c) steinmetz coefficient of material
(d) ambient temperature
28. Laminated cores, in electrical machines, are used to reduce
(a) copper loss
(b) eddy current loss
(c) hysteresis loss
(d) all of the above
1. A semiconductor is formed by .... bonds.
A] Covalent
B] Electrovalent
C] Co-ordinate
D] None of the above
2. A semiconductor has .... temperature coefficient of resistance.
A] Positive

B] Zero

C] Negative

D] None of the above

3. The most commonly used semiconductor is ....

A] Germanium

B] Silicon

C] Carbon

D] Sulphur

6. The resistivity of a pure silicon is about ....

A] 100 O cm

B] 6000 O cm

C] 3 x 105 O m

D] 6 x 10-8 O cm

7. When a pure semiconductor is heated, its resistance ....

A] Goes up

B] Goes down

C] Remains the same

D] Can't say

8. The strength of a semiconductor crystal comes from ....

A] Forces between nuclei

B] Forces between protons

C] Electron-pair bonds

D] None of the above

9. When a pentavalent impurity is added to a pure semiconductor, it becomes ....

A] An insulator

B] An intrinsic semiconductor

C] p-type semiconductor

D] n-type semiconductor

10. Addition of pentavalent impurity to a semiconductor createsmany ....

A] Free electrons

B] Holes

C] Valence electrons

D] Bound electrons

11. A pentavalent impurity has .... Valence electrons

A] 35

B] 4

C] 6

12. An n-type semiconductor is ....

A] Positively charged

B] Negatively charged

C] Electrically neutral

D] None of the above

14. Addition of trivalent impurity to a semiconductor creates many ....

A] Holes

B] Free electrons

C] Valence electrons

D] Bound electrons

15. A hole in a semiconductor is defined as ....

A] A free electron

B] The incomplete part of an electron pair bond

C] A free proton

D] A free neutron

16. The impurity level in an extrinsic semiconductor is about ..... of pure semiconductor.

A] 10 atoms for 108 atoms

B] 1 atom for 108 atoms

C] 1 atom for 104 atoms

D] 1 atom for 100 atoms

17. As the doping to a pure semiconductor increases, the bulk resistance of the semiconductor ....

A] Remains the same

B] Increases

C] Decreases

D] None of the above

18. A hole and electron in close proximity would tend to ....

A] Repel each other

B] Attract each other

C] Have no effect on each other

D] None of the above

19. In a semiconductor, current conduction is due to ....

A] Only holes

B] Only free electrons

C] Holes and free electrons

D] None of the above

20. The random motion of holes and free electrons due to thermal agitation is called ....

A] Diffusion

B] Pressure

C] Ionisation

D] None of the above

21. A forward biased pn junction diode has a resistance of the order of

A] Ok

B] O

C] MO

D] None of the above

22. The battery connections required to forward bias a pn junction are ......

A] +ve terminal to p and –ve terminal to n

B] -ve terminal to p and +ve terminal to n

C] -ve terminal to p and –ve terminal to n

D] None of the above

23. The barrier voltage at a pn junction for germanium is about ....

A] 5 V

B] 3 V

C] Zero

D] 3 V

24. In the depletion region of a pn junction, there is a shortage of ....

A] Acceptor ions

B] Holes and electrons

C] Donor ions

D] None of the above

25. A reverse bias pn junction has ....

A] narrow depletion layer

B] Almost no current

C] Very low resistance

D] Large current flow

26. A pn junction acts as a ....

A] Controlled switch

B] Bidirectional switch

C] Unidirectional switch

D] None of the above

27. A reverse biased pn junction has resistance of the order of

A] Ok
B] O
C] MO
D] None of the above

28. The leakage current across a pn junction is due to ....
A] Minority carriers
B] Majority carriers
C] Junction capacitance
D] None of the above

29. When the temperature of an extrinsic semiconductor is increased, the pronounced effect is on......
A] Junction capacitance
B] Minority carriers
C] Majority carriers
D] None of the above

30. With forward bias to a pn junction , the width of depletion layer ....
A] Decreases
B] Increases
C] Remains the same
D] None of the above

31. The leakage current in a pn junction is of the order of
A] Aa
B] mA
C] kA
D] μA

32. In an intrinsic semiconductor, the number of free electrons ....
A] Equals the number of holes
B] Is greater than the number of holes
C] Is less than the number of holes
D] None of the above

33. At room temperature, an intrinsic semiconductor has ....
A] Many holes only
B] A few free electrons and holes
C] Many free electrons only
D] No holes or free electrons

34. At absolute temperature, an intrinsic semiconductor has ....
A] A few free electrons
B] Many holes

C] Many free electrons

D] No holes or free electrons

35. At room temperature, an intrinsic silicon crystal acts approximately as ......

A] A battery

B] A conductor

C] An insulator

D] A piece of copper wire

1. A transistor has ....

A] one pn junction

B] two pn junctions

C] three pn junctions

D] four pn junctions

2. The number of depletion layers in a transistor is ....

A] four

B] three

C] one

D] two

3. The base of a transistor is .... doped

A] heavily

B] moderately

C] lightly

D] none of the above

4. The element that has the biggest size in a transistor is ....

A] collector

B] base

C] emitter

D] collector-base-junction

5. In a pnp transistor, the current carriers are ....

A] acceptor ions

B] donor ions

C] free electrons

D] holes

6. The collector of a transistor is .... doped

A] heavily

B] moderately

C] lightly

D] none of the above

7. A transistor is a .... operated device
A] current
B] voltage
C] both voltage and current
D] none of the above
8. In a npn transistor, ... are the minority carriers
A] free electrons
B] holes
C] donor ions
D] acceptor ions
9. The emitter of a transistor is .... doped
A] lightly
B] heavily
C] moderately
D] none of the above
10. In a transistor, the base current is about .... of emitter current
A] 25%
B] 20%
C] 35 %
D] 5%
11. At the base-emitter junctions of a transistor, one finds ....
A] a reverse bias
B] a wide depletion layer
C] low resistance
D] none of the above
12. The input impedance of a transistor is ....
A] high
B] low
C] very high
D] almost zero
13. Most of the majority carriers from the emitter ....
A] recombine in the base
B] recombine in the emitter
C] pass through the base region to the collector
D] none of the above
14. The current IB is ....
A] electron current
B] hole current

C] donor ion current

D] acceptor ion current

15. In a transistor ....

A] IC = IE + IB

B] IB = IC + IE

C] IE = IC – IB

D] IE = IC + IB

16. The value of a of a transistor is ....

A] more than 1

B] less than 1

C] 1

D] none of the above

17. IC = aIE + ...

A] IB

B] ICEO

C] ICBO

D] ßIB

18. The output impedance of a transistor is ....

A] high

B] zero

C] low

D] very low

19. In a tansistor, IC = 100 mA and IE = 100.2 mA. The value of ß is ....

A] 100

B] 50

C] about 1

D] 200

20. In a transistor if ß = 100 and collector current is 10 mA, then IE is ....

A] 100 mA

B] 100.1 mA

C] 110 mA

D] none of the above

21. The relation between ß and a is ....

A] ß = 1 / (1 – a)

B] ß = (1 – a) / a

C] ß = a / (1 – a)

D] ß = a / (1 + a)

22. The value of ß for a transistor is generally ....

A] 1less than 1

B] between 20 and 500

C] above 500

23. The most commonly used transistor arrangement is .... arrangement

A] common emitter

B] common base

C] common collector

D] none of the above

24. The input impedance of a transistor connected in ....arrangement is the highest

A] common emitter

B] common collector

C] common base

D] none of the above

25. The output impedance of a transistor connected in ....

A] arrangement is the highest

B] common emitter

C] common collector

D] common base

none of the above

26. The phase difference between the input and output voltages in a common base arrangement is ....

A] 180o

B] 90o

C] 270o

D] 0o

27. The power gain in a transistor connected in .... arrangement is the highest

A] common emitter

B] common base

C] common collector

D] none of the above

28. The phase difference between the input and output voltages of a transistor connected in common emitter arrangement is ....

A] 0o

B] 180o

C] 90o

D] 270o

29. The voltage gain in a transistor connected in .... arrangement is the highest

A] common base

B] common collector

C] common emitter

D] none of the above

30. As the temperature of a transistor goes up, the base-emitter resistance ....

A] decreases

B] increases

C] remains the same

D] none of the above

31. The voltage gain of a transistor connected in common collector

A] arrangement is ....

B] equal to 1

C] more than 10

D] more than 100 less than 1

32. The phase difference between the input and output voltages of a transistor connected in common collector arrangement is ....

A] 180o

B] 0o

C] 90o

D] 270o

33. IC = ß IB + ...

A] ICBO

B] IC

C] ICEO

D] aIE

34. IC = [a / (1 – a)] IB + ...

A] ICEO

B] ICBO

C] IC

D] (1 – a) IB

35. IC = [a / (1 – a)] IB + [........ / (1 – a)]

A] ICBO

B] ICEO
C] IC
D] IE
36. BC 147 transistor indicates that it is made of ....
A] germanium
B] silicon
C] carbon
D] none of the above
37. ICEO = (.........) ICBO
A] ß1
B] + a
C] 1 + ß
D] none of the above
38. A transistor is connected in CB mode. If it is not connected in CE mode with same bias voltages, the values of IE, IB and IC will ....
A] remain the same
B] increase
C] decrease
D] none of the above
39. If the value of a is 0.9, then value of ß is ....
A] 9
B] 0.9
C] 900
D] 90
40. In a transistor, signal is transferred from a .... circuit
A] high resistance to low resistance
B] low resistance to high resistance
C] high resistance to high resistance
D] low resistance to low resistance
41. The arrow in the symbol of a transistor indicates the direction of ....
A] electron current in the emitter
B] electron current in the collector
C] hole current in the emitter
D] donor ion current
42. The leakage current in CE arrangement is .... that in CB arrangement
A] more than

B] less than
C] the same as
D] none of the above
43. A heat sink is generally used with a transistor to ....
A] increase the forward current
B] decrease the forward current
C] compensate for excessive doping
D] <u>prevent excessive temperature rise</u>
44. The most commonly used semiconductor in the manufacture of a transistor is ....
A] germanium
B] <u>silicon</u>
C] carbon
D] none of the above
45. The collector-base junction in a transistor has ....
A] forward bias at all times
B] <u>reverse bias at all times</u>
C] low resistance
D] none of the above
1. A tuned amplifier uses .... load
A] Resistive
B] Capacitive
C] <u>LC tank</u>
D] Inductive
2. A tuned amplifier is generally operated in .... operation
A] Class A
B] <u>Class C</u>
C] Class B
D] None of the above
3. A tuned amplifier is used in .... applications
A] <u>Radio frequency</u>
B] Low frequency
C] Audio frequency
D] None of the above
4. Frequencies above .... kHz are called radio frequencies
A] 21
B] 0
C] 50

D] 200

6. The voltage gain of a tuned amplifier is .... at resonant frequency

A] Minimum

B] Maximum

C] Half-way between maximum and minimum

D] Zero

7. At parallel resonance, the line current is ....

A] Minimum

B] Maximum

C] Quite large

D] None of the above

8. At series resonance, the circuit offers .... impedance

A] Zero

B] Maximum

C] Minimum

D] None of the above

9. A resonant circuit contains .... elements

A] R and L only

B] R and C only

C] Only R

D] L and C

10. At series or parallel resonance, the circuit behaves as a .... load

A] Capacitive

B] Resistive

C] Inductive

D] None of the above

11. At series resonance, voltage across L is .... voltage across C

A] Equal to but opposite in phase to

B] Equal to but in phase with

C] Greater than but in phase with

D] Less than but in phase with

12. When either L or C is increased, the resonant frequency of LC circuit ....

A] Remains the same

B] Increases

C] Decreases

D] Insufficient data

13. At parallel resonance, the net reactive component circuit current is …………

A] Capacitive
B] Zero
C] Inductive
D] None of the above

14. In parallel resonance, the circuit impedance is …………..

A] C/LR
B] R/LC
C] CR/L
D] L/CR

15. In a parallel LC circuit, if the input signal frequency is increased above resonant frequency then ……………………

A] XL increases and XC decreases
B] XL decreases and XC increases
C] Both XL and XC increase
D] Both XL and XC decrease

16. The Q of an LC circuit is given by …………………

A] 2pfr x R
B] R / 2pfrL
C] 2pfrL / R
D] R2/2pfrL

17. If Q of an LC circuit increases, then bandwidth …………………

A] Increases
B] Decreases
C] Remains the same
D] Insufficient data

18. At series resonance, the net reactive component of circuit current is ……………….

A] Zero
B] Inductive
C] Capacitive
D] None of the above

19. The dimensions of L/CR are that of ……………

A] Farad
B] Henry
C] Ohm
D] None of the above

20. If L/C ratio of a parallel LC circuit is increased, the Q of the circuit ....

A] Is decreased

B] Is increased

C] Remains the same

D] None of the above

21. At series resonance, the phase angle between applied voltage and circuit is ....

A] 90o

B] 180o

C] 0o

D] None of the above

22. At parallel resonance, the ratio L/C is ....

A] Very large

B] Zero

C] Small

D] None of the above

23. If the resistance of a tuned circuit is increased, the Q of the circuit ....

A] Is increased

B] Is decreased

C] Remains the same

D] None of the above

24. The Q of a tuned circuit refers to the property of ....

A] Sensitivity

B] Fidelity

C] Selectivity

D] None of the above

25. At parallel resonance, the phase angle between the applied voltage and circuit current is ....

A] 90o

B] 180o

C] 0o

D] None of the above

26. In a parallel LC circuit, if the signal frequency is decreased below the resonant frequency, then ....

A] XL decreases and XC increases

B] XL increases and XC decreases

C] Line current becomes minimum

D] None of the above

27. In series resonance, there is ....

A] Voltage amplification

B] Current amplification

C] Both voltage and current amplification

D] None of the above

28. The Q of a tuned amplifier is generally ....

A] Less than 5

B] Less than 10

C] More than 10

D] None of the above

29. The Q of a tuned amplifier is 50. If the resonant frequency for the amplifier is 1000kHZ, then bandwidth is ....

A] 10kHz

B] 40 kHz

C] 30 kHz

D] 20 kHz

30. In the above question, what are the values of cut-off frequencies?

A] 140 kHz , 60 kHz

B] 1020 kHz , 980 kHz

C] 1030 kHz , 970 kHz

D] None of the above

31. For frequencies above the resonant frequency, a parallel LC circuit behaves as a .... load

A] Capacitive

B] Resistive

C] Inductive

D] None of the above

32. In parallel resonance, there is ....

A] Both voltage and current amplification

B] Voltage amplifications

C] Current amplification

D] None of the above

33. For frequencies below resonant frequency, a series LC circuit behaves as a .... load

A] Resistive

B] Capacitive

C] Inductive

D] None of the above

34. If a high degree of selectivity is desired, then double-tuned circuit should have .... coupling

A] Loose

B] Tight

C] Critical

D] None of the above

35. In the double tuned circuit, if the mutual inductance between the two tuned circuits is decreased, the level of resonance curve ....

A] Remains the same

B] Is lowered

C] Is raised

D] None of the above

36. For frequencies above the resonant frequency , a series LC circuit behaves as a .... load

A] Resistive

B] Inductive

C] Capacitive

D] None of the above

37. Double tuned circuits are used in .... stages of a radio receiver

A] IF

B] Audio

C] Output

D] None of the above

38. A class C amplifier always drives .... load

A] A pure resistive

B] A pure inductive

C] A pure capacitive

D] A resonant tank

39. Tuned class C amplifiers are used for RF signals of ....

A] Low power

B] High power

C] Very high power

D] None of the above

40. For frequencies below the resonant frequency , a parallel LC circuit behaves as a .... load

A] Inductive

B] Resistive

C] Capacitive

D] None of the above

1. A radio receiver has .... of amplification

A] One stage

B] Two stages

C] Three stages

D] More than one stages

2. RC coupling is used for .... amplification

A] Voltage

B] Current

C] Power

D] None of the above

3. In an RC coupled amplifier, the voltage gain over mid-frequency range ....

A] Changes abruptly with frequency

B] Is constant

C] Changes uniformly with frequency

D] None of the above

4. In obtaining the frequency response curve of an amplifier, the ....

A] Amplifier level output is kept constant

B] Amplifier frequency is held constant

C] Generator frequency is held constant

D] Generator output level is held constant

5. An advantage of RC coupling scheme is the ....Good impedance matching

A] Economy

B] High efficiency

C] None of the above

6. The best frequency response is of .... coupling

A] RC

B] Transformer

C] Direct

D] None of the above

7. Transformer coupling is used for .... amplification

A] Power

B] Voltage

C] Current

D] None of the above

8. In an RC coupling scheme, the coupling capacitor CC must be large enough ....

A] To pass d.c. between the stages

B] Not to attenuate the low frequencies

C] To dissipate high power

D] None of the above

9. In RC coupling, the value of coupling capacitor is about ....

A] 100 pF

B] 0.1 μF

C] 0.01 μF

D] 10 μF

11. When a multistage amplifier is to amplify d.c. signal, then one must use .... coupling

A] RC

B] Transformer

C] Direct

D] None of the above

12. .... coupling provides the maximum voltage gain

A] RC

B] Transformer

C] Direct

D] Impedance

13. In practice, voltage gain is expressed ....

A] In db

B] In volts

C] As a number

D] None of the above

14. Transformer coupling provides high efficiency because ....

A] Collector voltage is stepped up

B] resistance is low

C] collector voltage is stepped down

D] none of the above

15. Transformer coupling is generally employed when load resistance is ....

A] Large

B] Very large

C] Small

D] None of the above

16. If a three-stage amplifier has individual stage gains of 10 db, 5 db and 12 db, then total gain in db is ....

A] 600 db

B] 24 db

C] 14 db

D] 27 db

17. The final stage of a multistage amplifier uses ....

A] RC coupling

B] Transformer coupling

C] Direct coupling

D] Impedance coupling

18. The ear is not sensitive to ....

A] Frequency distortion

B] Amplitude distortion

C] Frequency as well as amplitude distortion

D] None of the above

19. RC coupling is not used to amplify extremely low frequencies because ....

A] There is considerable power loss

B] There is hum in the output

C] Electrical size of coupling capacitor becomes very large

D] None of the above

20. In transistor amplifiers, we use .... transformer for impedance matching

A] Step up

B] Step down

C] Same turn ratio

D] None of the above

21. The lower and upper cut off frequencies are also called .... frequencies

A] Sideband

B] Resonant

C] Half-resonant

D] Half-power

22. A gain of 1,000,000 times in power is expressed by ....

A] 30 db

B] 60 db

C] 120 db
D] 600 db
23. A gain of 1000 times in voltage is expressed by ....
A] 60 db
B] 30 db
C] 120 db
D] 600 db
24. 1 db corresponds to .... change in power level
A] 50%
B] 35%
C] 26%
D] 22%
25. 1 db corresponds to .... change in voltage or current level
A] 40%
B] 80%
C] 20%
D] 25%
26. The frequency response of transformer coupling is ....
A] Good
B] Very good
C] Excellent
D] Poor
27. In the initial stages of a multistage amplifier, we use ....
A] RC coupling
B] Transformer coupling
C] Direct coupling
D] None of the above
28. The total gain of a multistage amplifier is less than the product of the gains of individual stages due to ....
A] Power loss in the coupling device
B] Loading effect of the next stage
C] The use of many transistors
D] The use of many capacitors
29. The gain of an amplifier is expressed in db because ....
A] It is a simple unit
B] Calculations become easy
C] Human ear response is logarithmic
D] None of the above

30. If the power level of an amplifier reduces to half, the db gain will fall by ....

A] 5 db

B] 2 db

C] 10 db

D] 3 db

31. A current amplification of 2000 is a gain of ....

A] 3 db

B] 66 db

C] 20 db

D] 200 db

32. An amplifier receives 0.1 W of input signal and delivers 15 W of signal power. What is the power gain in db?

A] 8 db

B] 6 db

C] 5 db

D] 4 db

33. The power output of an audio system is 18 W. For a person to notice an increase in the output (loudness or sound intensity) of the system, what must the output power be increased to ?

A] 2 W

B] 6 W

C] 68 W

D] None of the above

34. The output of a microphone is rated at -52 db. The reference level is 1V under specified conditions. What is the output voltage of this microphone under the same sound conditions?

A] 5 mV

B] 2 mV

C] 8 mV

D] 5 mV

35. RC coupling is generally confined to low power applications because of ....

A] Large value of coupling capacitor

B] Low efficiency

C] Large number of components

D] None of the above

36. The number of stages that can be directly coupled is limited because ....

A] Changes in temperature cause thermal instability

B] Circuit becomes heavy and costly

C] It becomes difficult to bias the circuit

D] None of the above

37. The purpose of RC or transformer coupling is to ....

A] Block a.c.

B] Separate bias of one stage from another

C] Increase thermal stability

D] None of the above

38. The upper or lower cut off frequency is also called ....frequency

A] Resonant

B] Sideband

C] 3 db

D] None of the above

39. The bandwidth of a single stage amplifier is .... that of a multistage amplifier

A] More than

B] The same as

C] Less than

D] Data insufficient

40. The value of emitter capacitor CE in a multistage amplifier is about ....

A] 1 μF

B] 100 pF

C] 0.01 μF

D] 50 μF

1. A Triac has three terminals viz ....

1. Drain, source, gate

2. Two main terminal and a gate terminal

3. Cathode, anode, gate

4. None of the above

Ans : 2

2. A triac is equivalent to two SCRs ....

1. In parallel

2. In series

3. In inverse-parallel

4. None of the above
Ans : 3
3. A triac is a .... switch
1. Bidirectional
2. Unidirectional
3. Mechanical
4. None of the above
Ans : 1
4. The V-I characteristics for a triac in the first and third quadrants are essentially identical to those of .... in its first quadrant
1. Transistor
2. SCR
3. UJT
4. none of the above
Ans : 2
5. A triac can pass a portion of .... half-cycle through the load
1. Only positive
2. Only negative
3. Both positive and negative
4. None of the above
Ans : 3
6. A diac has .... terminals
1. Two
2. Three
3. Four
4. None of the above
Ans : 1
7. A triac has .... semiconductor layers
1. Two
2. Three
3. Four
4. Five
Ans : 3
8. A diac has .... pn junctions
1. Four
2. Two
3. Three
4. None of the above

Ans : 2

9. The device that does not have the gate terminal is ....

1. Triac
2. FET
3. SCR
4. Diac

Ans : 4

10. A diac has .... semiconductor layers

1. Three
2. Two
3. Four
4. None of the above

Ans : 1

11. A UJT has ....

1. Two pn junctions
2. One pn junction
3. Three pn junctions
4. None of the above

Ans : 2

12. The normal way to turn on a diac is by ....

1. Gate current
2. Gate voltage
3. Breakover voltage
4. None of the above

Ans : 3

13. A diac is .... switch

1. An c.
2. A d.c.
3. A mechanical
4. None of the above

Ans : 1

14. In a UJT, the p-type emitter is .... doped

1. Lightly
2. Heavily
3. Moderately
4. None of the above

Ans : 2

15. Power electronics essentially deals with control of a.c. power

at ....
1. Frequencies above 20 kHz
2. Frequencies above 1000 kHz
3. Frequencies less than 10 Hz
4. 50 Hz frequency
Ans : 4

16. When the emitter terminal of a UJT is open, the resistance between the base terminal is generally ....
1. High
2. Low
3. Extremely low
4. None of the above
Ans : 1

17. When a UJT is turned ON, the resistance between emitter terminal and lower base terminal ....
1. Remains the same
2. Is decreased
3. Is increased
4. None of the above
Ans : 2

18. To turn on UJT, the forward bias on the emitter diode should be .... the peak point voltage
1. Less than
2. Equal to
3. More than
4. None of the above
Ans : 3

19. A UJT is sometimes called .... diode
1. Low resistance
2. High resistance
3. Single-base
4. Double-base
Ans : 4

20. When the temperature increases, the inter-base resistance (RBB) of a UJT ....
1. Increases
2. Decreases
3. Remains the same

4. None of the above

Ans : 1

21. When the temperature increases, the intrinsic stand off ratio ....

1. Increases

2. Decreases

3. Essentially remains the same

4. None of the above

Ans : 3

22. Between the peak point and the valley point of UJT emitter characteristics we have .... region

1. Saturation

2. Negative resistance

3. Cut-off

4. None of the above

Ans : 2

24. A diac is turned on by ....

1. A breakover voltage

2. Gate voltage

3. Gate current

4. None of the above

Ans : 1

25. The device that exhibits negative resistance region is ....

1. Diac

2. Triac

3. Transistor

4. UJT

Ans : 4

26. The UJT may be used as ....

1. Am amplifier

2. A sawtooth generator

3. A rectifier

4. None of the above

Ans : 2

27. A diac is simply ....

1. A single junction device

2. A three junction device

3. A triac without gate terminal

4. None of the above

Ans : 3

28. After peak point, the UJT operates in the .... region

1. Cut-off

2. Saturation

3. Negative resistance

4. None of the above

Ans : 3

29. Which of the following is not a characteristic of UJT?

1. Intrinsic stand off ratio

2. Negative resistance

3. Peak-point voltage

4. Bilateral conduction

Ans : 4

30. The triac is ....

1. Like a bidirectional SCR

2. A four-terminal device

3. Not a thyristor

4. Answers (1) and (2)

Ans : 1

1.In which of the following base systems is 123 not a valid number?

(a) Base 10

(b) Base 16

(c)Base8

(d) Base 3

2. Storage of 1 KB means the following number of bytes

(a) 1000

(b)964

(c)1024

(d) 1064

3. What is the octal equivalent of the binary number:

10111101

(a)675

(b)275

(c) 572

(d) 573.

4. Pick out the CORRECT statement:

(a) In a positional number system, each symbol represents the same value irrespective of its position

(b) The highest symbol in a position number system as a value equal to the number of symbols in the system

(c) It is not always possible to find the exact binary

(d) Each hexadecimal digit can be represented as a sequence of three binary symbols.

5.The binary code of (21.125)10 is

(a) 10101.001

(b) 10100.001

(c) 10101.010

(d) 10100.111.

6.A NAND gate is called a universal logic element because

(a) it is used by everybody

(b) any logic function can be realized by NAND gates alone

(c) all the minization techniques are applicable for optimum NAND gate realization

(d) many digital computers use NAND gates.

7. Digital computers are more widely used as compared to analog computers,

because they are

(a) less expensive

(b) always more accurate and faster

(c) useful over wider ranges of problem types

(d) easier to maintain.

8. Most of the digital computers do not have floating point hardware because

(a) floating point hardware is costly

(b) it is slower than software

(c) it is not possible to perform floating point addition by hardware

(d) of no specific reason.

9. The number 1000 would appear just immediately after

(a) FFFF (hex)

(b) 1111 (binary)

(c) 7777 (octal)

(d) All of the above.

10. (1(10101)2 is

(a) (37)10

(b) (69)10

(c) (41)10

(d) — (5)10

11. The number of Boolean functions that can be generated by n variables is equal to

(a) 2n

(b) 22 n

(c) 2n-1

(d) — 2n

12. Consider the representation of six-bit numbers by two's complement, one's complement, or by sign and magnitude: In which representation is there overflow from the addition of the integers 011000 and 011000?

(a) Two's complement only

(b) Sign and magnitude and one's complement only

(c) Two's complement and one's complement only

(d) All three representations.

13. A hexadecimal odometer displays F 52 F. The next reading will be

(a)F52E

(b)G52F

(c)F53F

(d)F53O.

14. Positive logic in a logic circuit is one in which

(a) logic 0 and 1 are represented by 0 and positive voltage respectively

(b) logic 0 and, -1 are represented by negative and positive voltages respectively

(c) logic 0 voltage level is higher than logic 1 voltage level

(d) logic 0 voltage level is lower than logic 1 voltage level.

15. Which of the following gate is a two-level logic gate

(a) OR gate

(b) NAND gate

(c) EXCLUSIVE OR gate

(d) NOT gate.

16. Among the logic families, the family which can be used at very high frequency greater than 100 MHz in a 4 bit synchronous counter is

(a) TTLAS

(b) CMOS

(c)ECL

(d)TTLLS

17. An AND gate will function as OR if

(a) all the inputs to the gates are "1"

(b) all the inputs are '0'

(c) either of the inputs is "1"

(d) all the inputs and outputs are complemented.

18. An OR gate has 6 inputs. The number of input words in its truth table are

(a)6

(b)32

(c) 64

(d) 128

19. A debouncing circuit is

(a) an astable MV

(b) a bistable MV

(c) a latch

(d) a monostable MV.

20. NAND. gates are preferred over others because these

(a) have lower fabrication area

(b) can be used to make any gate

(c) consume least electronic power

(d) provide maximum density in a chip.

21. In case of OR gate, no matter what the number of inputs, a

(a) 1 at any input causes the output to be at logic 1

(b) 1 at any input causes the output to be at logic 0

(c) 0 any input causes the output to be at logic 0

(d) 0 at any input causes the output to be at logic 1.

22. The fan put of a 7400 NAND gate is

(a)2TTL

(b)5TTL

(c)8TTL

(d)10TTL

23. Excess-3 code is known as

(a) Weighted code

(b) Cyclic redundancy code

(c) Self-complementing code

(d) Algebraic code.

k24. Assuming 8 bits for data, 1 bit for parity, I start bit and 2 stop bits, the number of characters that 1200 BPS communication line can transmit is

(a)10 CPS

(b)120 CPS
(c) 12CPS
(d) None of the above.
1. The commercial sources of energy are
(a) solar, wind and biomass
(b) fossil fuels, hydropower and nuclear energy
(c) wood, animal wastes and agriculture wastes
(d) none of the above
3. In India largest thermal power station is located at
(a) Kota
(b) Sarni
(c) Chandrapur
(d) Neyveli
4. The percentage O2 by Weight in atmospheric air is
(a) 18%
(b) 23%
(c) 77%
(d) 79%
5. The percentage 02 by volume in atmosphere air is
(a) 21%
(b) 23%
(c) 77%
(d) 79%
6. The proper indication of incomplete combustion is
(a) high CO content in flue gases at exit
(b) high CO2 content in flue gases at exit
(c) high temperature of flue gases
(d) the smoking exhaust from chimney
7. The main source of production of biogas is
(a) human waste
(b) wet cow dung
(c) wet livestock waste
(d) all above
8. India's first nuclear power plant was installed at
(a) Tarapore
(b) Kota
(c) Kalpakkam
(d) none of the above

9. In fuel cell, the _______ energy is converted into electrical energy.

(a) mechanical

(b) chemical

(c) heat

(d) sound

10. Solar thermal power generation can be achieved by

(a) using focusing collector or heliostates

(b) using flat plate collectors

(c) using a solar pond

(d) any of the above system

51. In case of impulse steam turbine

(a) there is enthalpy drop in fixed and moving blades

(b) there is enthalpy drop only in moving blades

(c) there is enthalpy drop in nozzles

(d) none of the above

52. The pressure on the two sides of the impulse wheel of a steam turbine

(a) is same

(b) is different

(c) increases from one side to the other side

(d) decreases from one side to the other side

53. In De Laval steam turbine

(a) the pressure in the turbine rotor is approximately same as in con¬denser

(b) the pressure in the turbine rotor is higher than pressure in the con¬denser

(c) the pressure in the turbine rotor gradually decreases from inlet to exit from

condenser

(d) none from the above

54. Incase of reaction steam turbine

(a) there is enthalpy drop both in fixed and moving blades

(b) there is enthalpy drop only in fixed blades

(c) there is enthalpy drop only in moving blades

(d) none of the above

55. Curtis turbine is

(a) reaction steam turbine

(b) pressure velocity compounded steam turbine

(c) pressure compounded impulse steam turbine
(d) velocity compounded impulse steam turbine
56. Rateau steam turbine is
(a) reaction steam turbine
(b) velocity compounded impulse steam turbine
(c) pressure compounded impulse steam turbine
(d) pressure velocity compounded steam turbine
57. Parson's turbine is
(a) pressure compounded steam turbine
(b) simple single wheel, impulse steam turbine
(c) simple single wheel reaction steam turbine
(d) multi wheel reaction steam turbine
58. For Parson's reaction steam turbine, degree of reaction is
(a) 75%
(b) 100%
(c) 50%
(d) 60%
59. Reheat factor in steam turbines depends on
(a) exit pressure only
(b) stage efficiency only
(c) initial pressures and temperature only
(d) all of the above
60. The value of reheat factor normally varies from
(a) 0.5 to 0.6
(b) 0.9 to 0.95
(c) 1.02 to 1.06
(d) 1.2 to 1.6
61. Steam turbines are governed by the following methods
(a) Throttle governing
(b) Nozzle control governing
(c) By-pass governing
(d) all of the above
62. In steam turbines the reheat factor
(a) increases with the increase in number of stages
(b) decreases with the increase in number of stages
(c) remains same irrespective of number of stages
(d) none of the above

63. The thermal efficiency of the engine with condenser as compared to without

condenser, for a given pressure and temperature of steam, is

(a) higher

(b) lower

(c) same as long as initial pressure and temperature is unchanged

(d) none of the above

64. In jet type condensers

(a) cooling water passes through tubes and steam surrounds them

(b) steam passes through tubes and cooling water surrounds them

(c) steam and cooling water mix

(d) steam and cooling water do not mix

65. In a shell and tube surface condenser

(a) steam and cooling water mix to give the condensate

(b) cooling water passes through the tubes and steam surrounds them

(c) steam passes through the cooling tubes and cooling water surrounds them

(d) all of the above varying with situation

66. In a surface condenser if air is removed, there is

(a) fall in absolute pressure maintained in condenser

(b) rise in absolute pressure maintained in condenser

(c) no change in absolute pressure in the condenser

(d) rise in temperature of condensed steam

67. The cooling section in the surface condenser

(a) increases the quantity of vapour extracted along with air

(b) reduces the quantity of vapour extracted along with air

(c) does not affect vapour quantity extracted but reduces pump capacity of air

extraction pump

(d) none of the above

68. Edward's air pump

(a) removes air and also vapour from condenser

(b) removes only air from condenser

(c) removes only un-condensed vapour from condenser

(d) removes air alongwith vapour and also the condensed water from condenser

69. In a steam power plant, the function of a condenser is

(a) to maintain pressure below atmospheric to increase work output from the
primemover
(b) to receive large volumes of steam exhausted from steam prime mover
(c) to condense large volumes of steam to water which may be used again in boiler
(d) all of the above
70. In a regenerative surface condenser
(a) there is one pump to remove air and condensate
(b) there are two pumps to remove air and condensate
(c) there are three pumps to remove air, vapour and condensate
(d) there is no pump, the condensate gets removed by gravity
71. Evaporative type of condenser has
(a) steam in pipes surrounded by water
(b) water in pipes surrounded by steam
(c) either (a) or (b)
(d) none of the above
72. Pipes carrying steam are generally made up of
(a) steel
(b) cast iron
(c) copper
(d) aluminium
73. For the safety of a steam boiler the number of safety valves fitted are
(a) four
(b) three
(c) two
(d) one
74. Steam turbines commonly used in steam power station are
(a) condensing type
(b) non-condensing type
(c) none of the above
75. Belt conveyer can be used to transport coal at inclinations upto
(a) 30°
(b) 60°
(c) 80°
(d) 90°
76. The maximum length of a screw conveyer is about
(a) 30 metres

(b) 40 metres
(c) 60 metres
(d) 100 metres

77. The efficiency of a modern boiler using coal and heat recovery equipment is about
(a) 25 to 30%
(b) 40 to 50%
(c) 65 to 70%
(d) 85 to 90%

78. The average ash content in Indian coals is about
(a) 5%
(b) 10%
(c) 15%
(d) 20%

79. Load center in a power station is
(a) center of coal fields
(b) center of maximum load of equipments
(c) center of gravity of electrical system

80. Steam pressure in a steam power station, which is usually kept now-a-days is of the order of
(a) 20 kgf/cm2
(b) 50 kgf/cm2
(c) 100 kgf/cm2
(d) 150 kgf/cm2

81. Economisers improve boiler efficiency by
(a) 1 to 5%
(b) 4 to 10%
(c) 10 to 12%

82. The capacity of large turbo-generators varies from
(a) 20 to 100 MW
(b) 50 to 300 MW
(c) 70 to 400 MW
(d) 100 to 650 MW

83. Caking coals are those which
(a) burn completely
(b) burn freely

(c) do not form ash

(d) form lumps or masses of coke

84. Primary air is that air which is used to

(a) reduce the flame length

(b) increase the flame length

(c) transport and dry the coal

(d) provide air around burners for get¬ting optimum combustion

85. Secondary air is the air used to

(a) reduce the flame length

(b) increase the flame length

(c) transport and dry the coal

(d) provide air round the burners for getting optimum combustion

86. In coal preparation plant, magnetic separators are used to remove

(a) dust

(b) clinkers

(c) iron particles

(d) sand

88. Method which is commonly applied for unloading the coal for small power

plant is

(a) lift trucks

(b) coal accelerators

(c) tower cranes

(d) belt conveyor

89. Bucket elevators are used for

(a) carrying coal in horizontal direction

(b) carrying coal in vertical direction

(c) carrying coal in any direction

90. The amount of air which is supplied for complete combustion is called

(a) primary air

(b) secondary air

(c) tertiary air

91. In _______ system fuel from a central pulverizing unit is delivered to a bunker

and then to the various burners

(a) unit

(b) central

(c) none of the above

92. Under-feed stokers work best for _______ coals high in volatile matter and

with caking tendency

(a) anthracite

(b) lignite

(c) semibituminous and bituminous

93. Example of overfeed type stoker is

(a) chain grate

(b) spreader

(c) travelling grate

(d) all of the above

94. Where unpulverised coal has to be used and boiler capacity is large, the stoker

which is used is

(a) underfeed stoker

(b) overfeed stoker

(c) any

96. Blowing down of boiler water is the process

(a) to reduce the boiler pressure

(b) to increase the steam temperature

(c) to control the solid concentration in the boiler water by removing some of the

concentrated saline water

(d) none of the above

97. Deaerative heating is done to

(a) heat the water

(b) heat the air in the water

(c) remove dissolved gases in the water

98. Reheat factor is the ratio of

(a) isentropic heat drop to useful heat drop

(b) adiabatic heat drop to isentropic heat drop

(c) cumulative actual enthalpy drop for the stages to total is isentropic enthalpy

heat drop

100. Compounding of steam turbine is done for

(a) reducing the work done

(b) increasing the rotor speed

(c) reducing the rotor speed

(d) balancing the turbine

1. By which of the following systems electric power may be transmitted ?

(a) Overhead system

(b) Underground system

(c) Both (a) and (b)

(d) None of the above

2 are the conductors, which connect the consumer's terminals to the distribution

(a) Distributors

(b) Service mains

(c) Feeders

(d) None of the above

3. The underground system cannot be operated above

(a) 440 V

(b) 11 kV

(c) 33 kV

(d) 66 kV

4. Overhead system can be designed for operation up to

(a) 11 kV

(b) 33 kV

(c) 66 kV

(d) 400 kV

5. If variable part of annual cost on account of interest and depreciation on the capital outlay is equal to the annual cost of electrical energy wasted in the conductors, the total annual cost will be minimum and the corresponding size of conductor will be most economical. This statement is known as

(a) Kelvin's law

(b) Ohm's law

(c) Kirchhoffs law

(d) Faraday's law

6. The wooden poles well impregnated with creosite oil or any preservative compound have life

(a) from 2 to 5 years

(b) 10 to 15 years

(c) 25 to 30 years

(d) 60 to 70 years

7. Which of the following materials is not used for transmission and distribution of electrical power ?

(a) Copper

(b) Aluminium

(c) Steel

(d) Tungsten

8. Galvanised steel wire is generally used as

(a) stay wire

(b) earth wire

(c) structural components

(d) all of the above

9. The usual spans with R.C.C. poles are

(a) 40—50 meters

(b) 60—100 meters

(c) 80—100 meters

(d) 300—500 meters

10. The corona is considerably affected by which of the following ?

(a) Size of the conductor

(b) Shape of the conductor

(c) Surface condition of the conductor

(d) All of the above

11. Which of the following are the constants of the transmission lines ?

(a) Resistance

(b) Inductance

(c) Capacitance

(d) All of the above

12. 310 km line is considered as

(a) a long line

(b) a medium line

(c) a short line

(d) any of the above

13. The phenomenon qf rise in voltage at the receiving end of the open-circuited

or lightly loaded line is called the

(a) Seeback effect

(b) Ferranti effect

(c) Raman effect

(d) none of the above

14. The square root of the ratio of line impedance and shunt admittance is called the

(a) surge impedance of the line

(b) conductance of the line

(c) regulation of the line

(d) none of the above

15. Which of the following is the demerit of a 'constant voltage transmission system' ?

(a) Increase of short-circuit current of the system

(b) Availability of steady voltage at all loads at the line terminals

(c) Possibility of better protection for the line due to possible use of higher terminal reactants

(d) Improvement of power factor at times of moderate and heavy loads

(e) Possibility of carrying increased power for a given conductor size in case of long-distance heavy power transmission

17. The operating voltage of high voltage cables is up to

(a)l.lkV

(b)3.3kV

(c)6.6kV

(d)llkV

18. The operating voltage of supertension cables is up to

(a) 3.3 kV

(b) 6.6 kV

(c) 11 kV

(d) 33 kV

19. The operating voltage of extra high tension cables is upto

(a) 6.6 kV

(b) 11 kV

(c) 33 kV

(d) 66 kV

20. Which of the following methods is used for laying of underground cables ?

(a) Direct laying

(b) Draw-in-system

(c) Solid system

(d) All of the above

22. Due to which of the following reasons the cables should not be operated too hot ?

(a) The oil may loose its viscosity and it may start drawing off from higher levels

(b) Expansion of the oil may cause the sheath to burst

(c) Unequal expansion may create voids in the insulation which will lead to ionization

(d) All of the above

23. Which of the following D.C. distribution system is the simplest and lowest in first cost ?

(a) Radial system

(b) Ring system

(c) Inter-connected system

(d) None of the above

24. A booster is a

(a) series wound generator

(b) shunt wound generator

(c) synchronous generator

(d) none of the above

25. Besides a method of trial and error, which of the following methods is employed for solution of network problems in interconnected system ?

(a) Circulating current method

(b) Thevenin's theorem

(c) Superposition of currents

(d) All of the above

28. The voltage of the single phase supply to residential consumers is

(a) 110 V

(b) 210 V

(c) 230 V

(d) 400 V

29. Most of the high voltage transmission lines in India are

(a) underground

(b) overhead

(c) either of the above

(d) none of the above

30. The distributors for residential areas are

(a) single phase

(b) three-phase three wire

(c) three-phase four wire
(d) none of the above
32. High voltage transmission lines use
(a) suspension insulators
(b) pin insulators
(c) both (a) and (b)
(d) none of the above
33. Multicore cables generally use
(a) square conductors
(b) circular conductors
(c) rectangular conductors
(d) sector-shaped conductors
34. Distribution lines in India generally use
(a) wooden poles
(b) R.C.C. poles
(c) steel towers
(d) none of the above
35. The material commonly used for insulation in high voltage cables is
(a) lead
(b) paper
(c) rubber
(d) none of the above
36. The loads on distributors systems are generally
(a) balanced
(b) unbalanced
(c) either of the above
(d) none of the above
37. The power factor of industrial loads is generally
(a) unity
(b) lagging
(c) leading
(d) zero
38. Overhead lines generally use
(a) copper conductors
(b) all aluminium conductors
(c) A.C.S.R. conductors
(d) none of these
39. In transmission lines the cross-arms are made of

(a) copper
(b) wood
(c) R.C.C.
(d) steel
40. The material generally used for armour of high voltage cables is
(a) aluminium
(b) steel
(c) brass
(d) copper
42. The material commonly used for sheaths of underground cables is
(a) lead
(b) rubber
(c) copper
(d) iron
43. The minimum clearance between the ground and a 220 kV line is about
(a) 4.3 m
(b) 5.5 m
(c) 7.0 m
(d) 10.5 m
44. The spacing between phase conductors of a 220 kV line is approximately equal to
(a) 2 m
(b) 3.5 m
(c) 6 m
(d) 8.5 m
45. Large industrial consumers are supplied electrical energy at
(a) 400 V
(b) 11 kV
(c) 66 kV
(d) 400 kV
48. Transmitted power remaining the same, if supply voltage of a D.C. 2-wire
feeder is increased 100 percent, saving in copper is
(a) 25 percent
(b) 50 percent
(c) 75 percent
(d) 100 percent

49. A uniformly-loaded D.C. distributor is fed at both ends with equal voltages. As compared to a similar distributor fed at one end only, the drop at the middle point is

(a) one-fourth

(b) one-third

(c) one-half

(d) twice

50. As compared to a 2-wire D.C. distributor, a 3-wire distributor with same maximum voltage to earth uses only

(a) 31.25 percent of copper

(b) 33.3 percent of copper

(c) 66.7 percent of copper

(d) 125 percent of copper

51. Which of the following is usually not the generating voltage ?

(a) 6.6 kV

(b) 8.8 kV

(c) 11 kV

(d) 13.2 kV

52. For an overhead line, the surge impedance is taken as

(a) 20-30 ohms

(b) 70—80 ohms

(c) 100—200 ohms

(d) 500—1000 ohms

Ans: c

53. The presence of ozone due to corona is harmful because it

(a) reduces power factor

(b) corrodes the material

(c) gives odour

(d) transfer energy to the ground

54. A feeder, in a transmission system, feeds power to

(a) distributors

(b) generating stations

(c) service mains

(d) all of the above

55. The power transmitted will be maximum when

(a) corona losses are minimum

(b) reactance is high

(c) sending end voltage is more

(d) receiving end voltage is more

56. A 3-phase 4 wire system is commonly used on

(a) primary transmission

(b) secondary transmission

(c) primary distribution

(d) secondary distribution

57. Which of the following materials is used for overhead transmission lines ?

(a) Steel cored aluminium

(b) Galvanised steel

(c) Cadmium copper

(d) Any of the above

58. Which of the following is not a constituent for making porcelain insulators ?

(a) Quartz

(b) Kaolin

(c) Felspar

(d) Silica

59. There is a greater possibility of occurence of corona during

(a) dry weather

(b) winter

(c) summer heat

(d) humid weather

60. Which of the following relays is used on long transmission lines ?

(a) Impedance relay

(b) Mho's relay

(c) Reactance relay

(d) None of the above

61. The steel used in steel cored conductors is usually

(a) alloy steel

(b) stainless steel

(c) mild steel

(d) high speed steel

62. Which of the following distribution systems is more reliable ?

(a) Radial system

(b) Tree system

(c) Ring main system

(d) All are equally reliable

63. Which of the following characteristics should the line supports for transmission lines possess ?

(a) Low cost

(b) High mechanical strength

(c) Longer life

(d) All of the above

64. Transmission voltage of ll kV is normally used for distances upto

(a) 20—25 km

(b) 40—50 km

(c) 60—70 km

(d) 80—100 km

65. Which of the following regulations is considered best?

(a) 50%

(b) 20%

(c) 10%

(d) 2%

66. Skin effect is proportional to

(a) (conductor diameter)

(b) (conductor diameter)

(c) (conductor diameter)

(d) (conductor diameter)

67. A conductor, due to sag between two supports, takes the form of

(a) semi-circle

(b) triangle

(c) ellipse

(d) catenary

68. In AC.S.R. conductors, the insulation between aluminium and steel conductors is

(a) insulin

(b) bitumen

(c) varnish

(d) no insulation is required

69. Which of the following bus-bar schemes has the lowest cost ?

(a) Ring bus-bar scheme

(b) Single bus-bar scheme

(c) Breaker and a half scheme

(d) Main and transfer scheme

71. By which of the following methods string efficiency can be improved ?

(a) Using a guard ring
(b) Grading the insulator
(c) Using long cross arm
(d) Any of the above

72. In aluminium conductors, steel core is provided to
(a) compensate for skin effect
(b) neutralise proximity effect
(c) reduce line inductance
(d) increase the tensile strength

73. By which of the following a bus-bar is rated ?
(a) Current only
(b) Current and voltage
(c) Current, voltage and frequency
(d) Current, voltage, frequency and short time current

74. A circuit is disconnected by isolators when
(a) line is energized
(b) there is no current in the line
(c) line is on full load
(d) circuit breaker is not open

75. For which of the following equipment current rating is not necessary ?

(a) Circuit breakers
(b) Isolators
(c) Load break switch
(d) Circuit breakers and load break switches

76. In a substation the following equipment is not installed
(a) exciters
(b) series capacitors
(c) shunt reactors
(d) voltatre transformers

77. jCorona usually occurs when the electrostatic stress in air around the conductor exceeds
(a) 6.6 kV (r.m.s. value)/cm
(b) 11 kV (r.m.s. value)/cm
(c) 22 kV (maximum value)/cm
(d) 30 kV (maximum value)/cm

78. The voltage drop, for constant voltage transmission is compensated by installing

(a) inductors

(b) capacitors

(c) synchronous motors

(d) all of above

(e) none of the above

79. The use of strain type insulators is made where the conductors are

(a) dead ended

(b) at intermediate anchor towers

(c) any of the above

(d) none of the above

80. The current drawn by the line due to corona losses is

(a) non-sinusoidal

(b) sinusoidal

(c) triangular

(d) square

81. Pin type insulators are generally not used for voltages beyond

(a) 1 kV

(b) 11 kV

(c) 22 kV

(d) 33 kV

82. Aluminium has a specific gravity of

(a) 1.5

(b) 2.7

(c) 4.2

(d) 7.8

83. For transmission of power over a distance of 200 km, the transmission voltage should be

(a) 132 kV

(b) 66 kV

(c) 33 kV

(d) 11 kV

84. For aluminium, as compared to copper, all the following factors have higher values except

(a) specific volume

(b) electrical conductivity

(c) co-efficient of linear expansion

(d) resistance per unit length for same cross-section

85. Which of the following equipment, for regulating the voltage in distribution feeder, will be most economical ?

(a) Static condenser

(b) Synchronous condenser

(c) Tap changing transformer

(d) Booster transformer

86. In a tap changing transformer, the tappings are provided on

(a) primary winding

(b) secondary winding

(c) high voltage winding

(d) any of the above

87. Constant voltage transmission entails the following disadvantage

(a) large conductor area is required for same power transmission

(b) short-circuit current of the system is increased

(c) either of the above

(d) none of the above

88. On which of the following factors skin effect depends ?

(a) Frequency of the current

(b) Size of the conductor

(c) Resistivity of the conductor material

(d) All of the above

89. The effect of corona can be detected by

(a) presence of ozone detected by odour

(b) hissing sound

(c) faint luminous glow of bluish colour

(d) all of the above

90. For transmission of power over a distance of 500 km, the transmission voltage should be in the range

(a) 150 to 220 kV

(b) 100 to 120 kV

(c) 60 to 100 kV

(d) 20 to 50 kV

91. In the analysis of which of the following lines shunt capacitance is neglected ?

(a) Short transmission lines

(b) Medium transmission lines

(c) Long transmission lines

(d) Medium as well as long transmission lines

92. When the interconnector between two stations has large reactance

(a) the transfer of power will take place with voltage fluctuation and noise

(b) the transfer of power will take place with least loss

(c) the stations will fall out of step be¬cause of large angular displacement between the stations

(d) none of the above

93. The frequency of voltage generated, in case of generators, can be increased by

(a) using reactors

(b) increasing the load

(c) adjusting the governor

(d) reducing the terminal voltage

(e) none of the above

94. When an alternator connected to the bus-bar is shut down the bus-bar voltage will

(a) fall

(b) rise

(c) remain unchanged

(d) none of the above

95. The angular displacement between two interconnected stations is mainly due to

(a) armature reactance of both alternators

(b) reactance of the interconnector

(c) synchronous reactance of both the alternators

(d) all of the above

96. Electro-mechanical voltage regulators are generally used in

(a) reactors

(b) generators

(c) transformers

(d) all of the above

97. Series capacitors on transmission lines are of little use when the load VAR requirement is

(a) large

(b) small

(c) fluctuating

(d) any of the above

98. The voltage regulation in magnetic amplifier type voltage regulator is effected by

(a) electromagnetic induction

(b) varying the resistance

(c) varying the reactance

(d) variable transformer

99. When a conductor carries more current on the surface as compared to core, it is due to

(a) permeability variation

(b) corona

(c) skin effect

(d) unsymmetrical fault

(e) none of the above

100. The following system is not generally used

(a) 1-phase 3 wire

(b) 1-phase 4 wire

(c) 3-phase 3 wire

(d) 3-phase 4 wire

www.ingramcontent.com/pod-product-compliance
Ingram Content Group UK Ltd.
Pitfield, Milton Keynes, MK11 3LW, UK
UKHW021917190726
13853UKWH00002B/709